Raoul Millais

Raoul Millais
HIS LIFE AND WORK

DUFF HART-DAVIS

SWAN·HILL
PRESS

By the same author

Behind the Scenes on a Newspaper
Ascension: the Story of the South Atlantic Island
Peter Fleming: a Biography
Monarchs of the Glen
Hitler's Games: the 1936 Olympics
Armada
Wildings: the Secret Garden of Eileen Soper
The House the Berrys Built
Country Matters (collected articles)
Further Country Matters
When the Country Went to Town

NOVELS

The Megacull
The Gold of St Matthew
Spider in the Morning
The Heights of Rimring
Level Five
Fire Falcon
The Man-Eater of Jassapur
Horses of War

First published in the UK in 1998
by Swan Hill Press, an imprint of Airlife Publishing Ltd

British Library Cataloguing-in-Publication Data
A catalogue record for this book
is available from the British Library

ISBN 1 85310 977 0

Typeset by Phoenix Typesetting, Ilkley, West Yorkshire
Printed in Italy

Swan Hill Press
an imprint of Airlife Publishing Ltd
101 Longden Road, Shrewsbury, SY3 9EB, England

ACKNOWLEDGEMENTS

My principal debt is to Raoul Millais himself, who put all his own writing at my disposal and stood up to prolonged interrogation with the good nature and fortitude of a man half his age. Other members of the family – his sons John, Hugh and Hexie, his grandson Colin and his stepdaughter Karol – have been unfailingly helpful.

Without the expertise of Raoul's grandson Joshua Lees-Millais, a professional photographer, it would have been impossible, and prohibitively expensive, to assemble colour transparencies of the paintings.

I also received valuable assistance from Brian Booth, Brigid Brett, Willie Carson, Lady Mary Clive, Ruth, Lady Dulverton, James Dunsmure, Sir Michael and Lady Farquhar, Sir Robert Fellowes, Christopher Fleming, Lady Mary Keen, Peter Metcalfe, Lord Oaksey, John and Diana Seymour-Williams, Anthony Sheil, Drusilla and Milton Shulman and the Hon. R. Wills.

Finally I should like to thank the Fine Arts Society Gallery, the National Horseracing Museum at Newmarket, the Royal Academy Schools and the Tryon Gallery for help in identifying horses, dates and paintings.

CONTENTS

PREFACE

The subject of this short memoir should really have written the book himself. Over his ninety-six years Raoul Millais has put thousands of words on paper, recounting episodes in his life, describing his family and upbringing, recalling friends, ridiculing the pretensions of modern art. He has also fired off any number of letters, many highly amusing. Yet as an author he has proved a sprinter rather than a stayer: he has never managed to draw all his reminiscences together into a single narrative – and in any case he has always been far too modest to give an objective account of his career.

The truth is that he has been one of the outstanding sporting artists of this century, and it has fallen to me to create some record of his achievement. Readers should be aware, however, that I have taken much of the text straight from Raoul's own writings; thus the chances are that if the occasional felicitous phrase gives pleasure, it is almost certainly his rather than mine.

When confronted with a single-page document authorising me to write the book, provisionally called *Raoul Millais*, he signed the agreement, but typically scribbled on the bottom: 'Don't much care for the title.'

DUFF HART-DAVIS

CHAPTER ONE

CHILDHOOD

On 15 May 1994, at the age of ninety-three, Raoul Millais wrote the following letter to Mike Farquhar and his wife Veronica, always known as Wong, who for the past few years had been framing his pictures, and had just held a successful exhibition at their home in Wiltshire:

An inadequate line of thanks for your amazing gifts of salesmanship, whereby you managed to palm off a quantity of my daubs (previously rejected by the Royal Academy Summer Exhibition) on to gullible customers from the more select corners of the Cotswolds and what was once our far-flung empire.

I feel I must however point out that we may be in the wrong business. A brother-brush called Mr Damien Hirst has just sold a disembowelled sheep suspended in a glass case and immersed in formaldehyde for £25,000 to a cultural and far-seeing client. Do you think that, next year, we might change our image?

I have first refusal of a hippo which died in the London Zoo last week from a surfeit of dough-nuts and hamburgers donated by visitors and their offspring. We could have it stuffed by a taxidermist and float it in vodka in a double-glazed swimming-pool, possibly painted shocking pink. I have a strong feeling that this significant statement might fetch £100,000 or more, and we could all have a weekend at Clacton-on-Sea.

Yr constant admirer, Charlie Creep (Failed RA).

The vitality and humour of the letter speak for themselves; how

Raoul's grandfather, Sir John Everett Millais, born in 1829, won a gold medal at the Royal Academy Schools at the age of eleven, and in 1848 joined Holman Hunt to found the Pre-Raphaelite movement. He died in 1896.

many men in their nineties spark with such ebullience? Yet the document hints at several other elements in the character of its extraordinary author. The most genuinely modest of artists, the least competitive and mercenary, Raoul Millais has persistently underrated his own skill as painter and draughtsman; being generous to a fault, he has given away hundreds of pictures, and has always been reluctant to sell his own works. In an active career spanning more than seventy years, he has held only four one-man exhibitions in London: at the Fine Arts Society's galleries in 1928 and 1936, and at the Tryon Gallery in 1973 and 1982. (Another show was held at the Tryon in 1991, but only four works came directly from him: the rest had been bought back from a collector in Suffolk.)

Yet at the same time he has always maintained a high regard for traditional artistic achievement, and scathing contempt for latter-day practitioners who pile bricks in heaps or dribble red paint indiscriminately over boards. As for the signature, some such wry twist ends many of his letters, and hints at his long-running feud with the Royal Academy, the august body of which his grandfather had been President.

Heredity dealt Raoul a strong hand; from his immediate fore-bears he derived many advantages. His height (6ft 4in), his slim build, his commanding good looks, his tremendous energy, his perfect manners, his love of the country and rural sports, his elegance on horseback and with a shotgun, his irrepressible sense of humour (which still often operates at prep-school level), above all his ability to draw and paint – all these were handed down by his grandfather, the distinguished artist Sir John Everett Millais, and his father, John Guille Millais, naturalist, big-game hunter, explorer, gardener, artist and author.

From his father also came those elements of character that have made him a lifelong loner. From an early age Raoul realised that he was not cut out to conform: over the years he has described himself as a misfit, a freak, a one-off, a do-it-yourself man, an 'enigma with perhaps too many variations'. Being blessedly free of ambition, he has never felt the need to compete or achieve ephemeral notoriety. Rather, he has gone his own way and consistently settled for 'the enjoyment of not worrying about being twelfth man in the side'. He has concentrated on the skills at which he excels: the painting and drawing of animals – horses above all – and the depiction of landscape and wild country.

The Millais family came from Jersey, where they were granted land by William the Conqueror because (according to Raoul) one of them had fought with him at Hastings 'and didn't actually run away'. They occupied the same house, Le Manoir de Tapon, from about 1300 until 1826, when the building burned to the ground: and in Raoul's words they kept out of financial trouble 'by consistently marrying heiresses and the daughters of Church dignitaries'.

Raoul never knew his grandfather, who died before he was born: but as he grew up, he gradually became aware that John Everett Millais had been a pillar of the Victorian art world. Born in 1829, he was extraordinarily precocious: he began drawing furiously at the age of four, and won a Gold Medal at the Royal Academy when he was only eleven. In 1848, still only nineteen, he and his friend William Holman Hunt founded the movement known as the Pre-Raphaelites, who rejected all forms of modernism in art and sought a return to nature. Then in 1855 he married Effie Gray, the divorced wife of the critic John Ruskin – an act which, in the repressive atmosphere of the day, demanded courage and determination from both parties. (Whereas Ruskin, it was alleged, had failed to consummate his marriage, Effie bore Millais eight children.)

Later J.E. was instrumental in persuading the London County Council to put up the money for Adrian Jones's great bronze statue of the Winged Victory driving a chariot which dominates Hyde Park Corner. He also persuaded Henry Tate, the sugar merchant, to finance the Tate Galley, and in the last year of his life, 1896,

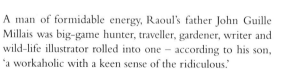

A man of formidable energy, Raoul's father John Guille Millais was big-game hunter, traveller, gardener, writer and wild-life illustrator rolled into one – according to his son, 'a workaholic with a keen sense of the ridiculous.'

became President of the Royal Academy. Art apart, he was a keen rider to hounds, shot, deer-stalker and fisherman; in his youth, around the 1850s, he hunted in Leicestershire with his friend the cartoonist John Leech, and later for many years rented two beats on the River Tay. His energy was legendary: he could jump his own height – 6ft 2in – and with very little provocation would do so in any host's drawing room after dinner.

His fourth son, John Guille, born in 1865 and always known as Johnny, was even more a man of the great outdoors. At Marlborough he would slip away from school to poach rabbits with his catapult in Savernake Forest. Even then he was gripped by an insatiable wanderlust, and later in life he travelled in many wild parts of the world. He was the first man to map the interior of Newfoundland, and hunted extensively in Africa, America, Alaska and Europe. He was also a keen and skilful gardener, and won the Gold Medal of the Horticultural Society. According to Raoul, he was 'enormously intelligent, with the energy of a racing car, a workaholic with immense enthusiasm and a keen sense of the ridiculous'.

In 1893 he married Fanny (Frances) Skipwith, the tall, slim and lively daughter of a Lincolnshire landowner. Their first child, Daphne, was born in 1895, followed by Geoffroy in 1896. For some years the couple lived in a rented house, but in 1900 they built a home of their own, Compton's Brow, a couple of miles north of Horsham, in Sussex. By then Fanny knew all too well that, like Tennyson's Ulysses, her husband could not rest from travel: he was for ever on his wanderings, often for months at a time; and when he did come home, he would immerse himself in writing and illustrating his latest book.

Like his energy and industry, the range of his interests seemed endless; big-game, deer, waterfowl, bats, seals – he studied, wrote about and drew creatures of every kind with limitless enthusiasm, establishing a reputation not only as a distinguished naturalist, but also as one of the leading wildlife illustrators of the day. The collection of African and North American big-game heads which he assembled in the specially built museum attached to Compton's Brow became the best in the world. The exhibits included a whole grizzly bear and, in two glass cases, a Pacific salmon weighing 60lb and a Tay salmon weighing 50lb. John Rigby, the rifle-maker, often came down, as did the taxidermist Rowland Ward, who mounted most of the heads.

The Millais' third child was born on 4 October 1901, and christened – with a resounding echo of the clan's Channel Island origins – Hesketh Raoul Lejarderay. He was followed, in 1904, by Rosamund, but only two years later the family was shocked by the sudden demise of Daphne, who fell ill with appendicitis and died after an operation at the age of eleven.

Raoul's earliest recollection is of a fierce nanny, 'a large woman with a heavy cavalry moustache and a hot temper', who was fond of Rosamund – a relatively docile character – but found two children a bit too much to handle. The result was that Raoul spent many hours locked in an attic box room, with strict instructions to keep still. The nanny threatened that if he moved about, ghosts would come through the creaking door which separated his prison from a black hole under the eaves containing the water tanks. He has never forgotten how he sat on a hard chair in the cold evening gloom which filtered through a skylight, waiting for the dreaded apparitions to appear. Yet by the time he was five or six he had worked out a means of keeping the demons at bay: he always managed to smuggle a piece of pencil or crayon into his cell, and stood on the chair to draw on the pink plaster walls, illustrating the fairy stories which his mother read to the children after tea.

Even at the age of six Raoul had a horror of deliberate cruelty, and the sight of someone inflicting punishment on an animal would send him into an uncontrollable rage. One winter day the nanny was pushing Rosamund in her pram, with Raoul hanging onto one side, for their afternoon walk through the village, when the milkman came along with his horse and cart. As he passed, the horse slipped on the icy surface and came down heavily, breaking one of the shafts – whereupon the milkman seized his whip and began to thrash the poor animal as it lay on the ground.

Raoul, screaming and crying, rushed at him, grabbed the whip and hit him in the face as hard as he could with the butt end. The boy's hysterical shrieks brought people out of their houses, while the milkman sat in the road with blood pouring from his nose, uttering fearful threats. Nanny dragged Raoul off, and all the way home promised dire retribution, but when Johnny heard what had happened, far from being angry with his son, he took him on his lap and said, 'Well done. If I'd been there, I'd have killed the fellow.'

In retrospect, Raoul felt that this was the moment when he realised for the first time that he loved his father. For many years he saw little of him yet, as he remembered later, 'he became for me a guiding light, although often only a pin-point in the darkness, as he was so often away in remote corners of the world'.

Seventy years later, Raoul wrote, 'If father had a weakness, it was that he fancied himself an expert on Old Masters.' On Wednesdays Johnny would have himself driven up to London, spend the morning at Sotheby's or Christie's, and return with a masterpiece, lamenting that it was an extravagance he could not afford. 'By Jove, I've got a Rubens!' he would cry. 'I've just bought a Constable.'

Sometimes Geoff and Raoul would offer him ten of the rabbits they had shot for his latest bargain, and he took the jests in good part. How the family remained solvent, Raoul could never make out, but he came to realise that his father was 'the con-man's dream' – a peculiar mixture of indomitable physical toughness and a touching faith in the honesty of others.

In due course the ferocious nanny was succeeded by another martinet, a German governess called Miss Buschell. Raoul spent countless hours writing out, 'I must not bite Miss Buschell' twenty-five times over – but his discomfiture was brought to a swift end by Geoff who, arriving back from school and taking an instant dislike to the lady, surreptitiously accelerated her descent of the precipitous back stairs. When she left, nursing a badly sprained wrist, there was great rejoicing in the Millais household.

The next governess was entirely different: a sweet little spinster called Miss Martin, who had faded auburn hair and thick spectacles, and twittered nervously like a sparrow. Wild flowers were her great passion; she was immensely knowledgeable about them, and when she took the children for walks in the country, she always carried a black tin for collecting specimens. It was she who suggested that Raoul should do illustrations for Longfellow's epic poem *Hiawatha*, and the enthusiasm with which she applauded his pictures gave him a strong push along the road to becoming a professional artist. Small wonder that, when she left, there were tears on both sides.

To Raoul, as a boy, Compton's Brow seemed 'like Clapham Junction', full of interesting people constantly coming and going. Gardeners, bird-watchers, naturalists, painters and writers all swept through the premises in hordes. Among them were his godfathers, the great big-game hunter Frederick Courteney Selous and Archibald Thorburn, the celebrated painter of birds – according to Raoul 'the best type of Scotsman' and a close friend of the family. Thorburn lived at Hascombe, near Godalming; like Johnny, he was tremendously industrious, and the two produced several books together.

Another frequent visitor was the author and journalist Hilaire Belloc, who came to dinner once a month when Johnny was at home. His host was a teetotaller, but Belloc drank beer by the gallon and would sit up until 2 a.m., roaring with laughter at his own jokes as he composed *Cautionary Tales* and other verses. Twice the family was threatened with a visit from King George V, who expressed a wish to see Johnny's trophies. Since he was known to be a voracious collector of big-game heads, the boys were enlisted to pre-empt him by carrying off their father's finest specimens to the bottom of the garden, but fortunately the monarch never came.

Whenever Johnny was in England, he did what he could to look after the children, and he passed on to his sons his own love of the wild. Among numerous other skills, he was amazingly accurate with shotgun, rifle and catapult. Every Christmas he would open the far window in the long drawing-room, place a lighted candle on the sill, walk back to the entrance door and shoot out the flame with a pellet from a catapult, usually at the first attempt.

He taught the boys a vast amount of country lore. By the time Raoul was ten he could make catapults out of forked privet branches, baked in the oven for twenty-four hours and fitted with elastic. He could shoot with various types of gun, hock and skin rabbits without a knife, set snares for rats with bent willow sticks and double horsehair nooses, snatch salmon, tickle trout and stalk pike with a snare dangling from the tip of a salmon rod. Further, he could recognise not only every common species of bird, but also their songs, including those of the warblers, which to most people are indistinguishable.

Animals played a large part in Raoul's childhood, not least a black and white rabbit called John Bunyan, who spent much of his time loose in the house, drank Earl Grey tea (never Indian), went for walks with the boys and became the inseparable companion of their father's black labrador, Flapper. Tragedy threatened early in his career when J.B. launched himself out of the nursery window on the top storey and smashed down onto crazy paving, breaking both forelegs and his jaw; yet devoted nursing brought him through this crisis and he survived for more than three years.

From their father the boys learned self-reliance, and also the need to judge people from all walks of life on their behaviour rather than on background or colour. Johnny always used to say that his two best friends were a duke and a shoemaker in Stromness, in Orkney; and later in life Raoul, who was himself absolutely without side, never ceased to be amazed by the subservience and awe bestowed upon the owners of titles.

During their father's long absences abroad, Geoff and Raoul would take to the wilds after their own fashion, hunting and camping in the 700 acres of St Leonard's Forest which Johnny had bought. The shoot, about two miles from home, harboured a few pheasants and partridges and hundreds of rabbits, and included two lakes. The preserve was guarded by a gipsy gamekeeper called George Smith, a former heavyweight boxer who wore rings in his ears and was the terror of local poachers. To the boys, this huge, dark man was the romantic protector of their forest, and at night they would sit for hours round the camp-fire, spellbound by his stories of life on the open road, told in a rich Sussex accent. It was he who taught Raoul how to set night lines for fish, how to squeal up a stoat within range by blowing on a blade of grass, and many other secrets.

The boys would walk out from home burdened with tent and sleeping-bags. Once on the ground, they were up with the light and spent most of their time ferreting rabbits, which they shot as they bolted from the burrows. (Raoul had a single-barrelled .410, Geoff a hammer 20-bore with Damascus barrels.) On one memo-rable day they killed seventy, and sold the lot to a local butcher for the then-princely sum of 2s 6d apiece – after which they thought themselves millionaires. Sometimes they carried off potatoes and asparagus in raids on the kitchen garden, and Gertie the cook would slip them eggs and bread from the kitchen; but they mostly fed themselves, cooking what they killed on an open fire. One winter, when Raoul shot a Canada goose in a snowstorm, the bird kept them going for days.

One of their secret weapons was a stuffed owl known as Jim, which, though moth-eaten, proved an irresistible provocation to magpies and crows. By perching him on a post in the forest and lying in wait, the boys were able to kill any number of egg-thieves and chick-snatchers, to the benefit of the songbird population. Another useful decoy was their heavyweight tomcat Buster, who was amazingly impervious to gunfire: even when magpies mobbing him came under bombardment from Raoul's .410, he would continue to swipe furiously at the attackers.

For boys with an outdoor bent, the shoot was paradise. The Romans had once exploited the underlying ironstone, and still the stream ran red as rust. Also red were the spotted toadstools which grew in profusion, and on which Raoul was convinced gnomes and elves sat to eat their hazelnuts. The boys often came upon skulls and bones, which their father identified as those of foxes or badgers, and sometimes the dogs found a hedgehog, which they took home wrapped in a handkerchief to release in the garden.

On Sundays, when shooting was forbidden, they had to devise other forms of entertainment and held long discussions about possible alternatives. One idea which appealed was to drain the top lake on the shoot – so they opened the sluice and released what seemed to be tons of eels and coarse fish down the stream which ran into the lake below. They thought this was a clever way of stocking the lower fishery, but the expanse of mud they created looked dreadful, and for days they remained in agonies of suspense lest somebody should realise who had created it.

Next they hit on the idea of ferreting mice with bumble-bees. A large grass bank was pock-marked with mouse-holes, and it was no problem to catch a few bumble-bees and keep them in match-boxes. But what could they use as purse-nets? The answer lay in a drawer of their mother's dressing table. While Raoul kept guard on the stairs, Geoff crept into her bedroom and borrowed a handful of her hair-nets. Placed over the holes, these proved very effective. Angry bees disappeared down the tunnels with loud boomings, and jet-propelled mice began popping out into the nets. The boys collapsed with laughter, but recovered in time to release their victims unharmed. The fragile nets, however, were in a bad way, and even though Geoff managed to smuggle them back without being detected, their mother inevitably noticed the damage. 'Boys,' she announced next day, 'it's most odd: something's been eating my hair-nets. I think it must be mice, and I want you to set some traps.'

Raoul adored Geoff, but he was also in awe of him. The elder brother grew into a formidable character – in his teens he was 6ft 4in tall, unafraid of anyone or anything, and immensely strong. Once after an argument, Raoul was walking away from him when he felt a sharp sting, between his shoulder blades.

'Keep still!' Geoff ordered. He had thrown a dart with some force into his brother's back, and as he pulled it out he said, 'If you tell father, I'll kill you.' Much as Raoul loved him, he was never sure whether or not Geoff would have carried out his threat.

When their faithful spaniel Smut picked up poison and died, Geoff soon thought up a new method of flushing rabbits from the dense undergrowth. 'Put this lot on,' he told Raoul, producing a pair of thick hedging gloves, leggings and a hood of some evil-smelling material in which he had cut two eye-holes. 'All you need do is crawl into the bushes and make a hell of a noise, like Smut did.'

By midday Raoul's clothes were in tatters, and so was much of his person. Geoff congratulated him on his performance so far, but when he suggested they should try the gorse bushes on the far side of the lake, Raoul's nerve broke. He bolted for home, where his appearance so horrified May, his mother's maid, that she forced him straight into a hot bath. When Geoff reappeared, and found his younger brother covered in plaster crosses, he merely said, 'You all right? Why on earth did you run off like that? Spoilt the whole day.'

Raoul was able to stuff any creature he caught, and set out to acquire specimens of all thirteen varieties of British bat. After a few years he had twelve, all carefully skinned, cured with alum and neatly pinned out in a showcase. One species, however, had eluded him: Bechstein's bat, which was pitch black and common in Germany, but exceedingly rare in England. His father told him he would never find one and advised him to stop trying; but then one day he was poking about in an old boathouse by the top lake on

Raoul's mother Fanny: this striking portrait, which he painted in oils at the age of nineteen, caught some of the strain and sadness engendered by his father's long absences abroad on shooting expeditions and botanical forays.

the shoot. Spotting the domed nest of a long-tailed tit on one of the beams, he put a finger into the hole at the side, felt something furry, brought it out and realised that he had hit on his missing link. Only a dedicated collector or naturalist could understand the excitement that gripped him. (Years later he presented the collection to the Natural History Museum in London.)

At home, Raoul and Geoff spent hours devising torments with which to bait the gardener, Mr Dooley, a crabby old man and a dedicated regular at the Horse & Jockey, the pub in the village. They stalked him with home-made bows and arrows, and as he bent over his vegetables they shot him in the backside with fine pellets from their catapults. Such minor aggravations he could tolerate; but when he found them digging up his asparagus bed for worms, it was too much. He reported them to their father, who promptly confiscated all weapons and fishing tackle for a week – a bitter blow.

The boys retaliated by preparing a special brew for Mr Dooley; a concoction of boiled berberis berries topped up with a measure of deadly nightshade and laced with brown sugar to disguise the taste. This they presented to him in a bottle bearing an old claret label filched from the cellar, and the gardener thanked them warmly, remarking, 'I ain't never tasted this Frenchified stuff afore.'

Next day, to their horror, he did not appear. On the second day he was absent again, and they rushed into the village, to find the door of his cottage locked. Convinced that they had killed him, they anxiously questioned anyone who might have seen him about. After desperate conferences about what to do, they discussed the possibility of running away to sea, and formed a definite plan for vanishing into the forest, should the police arrive. Fortunately their father was engrossed in the composition of a new book and noticed nothing unusual. Nor did their mother, except to ask occasionally if they were feeling sick – which indeed they were.

Their nerves were at breaking point when Mr Dooley suddenly appeared at the back door of the house, smelling strongly of the demon alcohol, and announced, 'I've been off to Bognor to bury me sister. I was sent for in an 'urry, and 'adn't the time to tell no one.' With that he moved off into the garden, but after a few steps he turned back and asked, ''Aven't got no more of that there Frenchified wine, 'ave yer? Arr, that were good stuff.'

So independent was Raoul that his father's long absences did not worry him. The person who suffered most was his mother, Fanny. As a young man he realised that she had been made wretched by loneliness and he came to see her as a tragic figure, a typical victim of a restrictive Victorian upbringing. At home, her distress was compounded by the fact that Geoff and Rosamund resented her fixed views and constantly argued with her. Raoul, ground between opposing forces as he tried to keep the peace, was often horrified to find her in tears.

With her good looks and excellent figure, Fanny remained attractive; but in those days of strict convention it was unthinkable that she should seek solace with some other man. Instead, she buried herself in gardening and social visits. The grounds of Compton's Brow were enormous. Out of the surrounding fields and forest Johnny had made a 12-acre garden, devoted mainly to rhododendrons, azaleas and magnolias, of which he and his friend Sir Edmund Loder created several new species by cross-pollination. Observing how droves of dedicated horticulturalists were escorted round in summer, Geoff and Raoul decided to test the temperament of visitors by hanging labels of their own invention on the bushes: *Blowdifinodea*, *Hilariosa*, *Insignifica*. In a show of irritation their father confiscated their guns for a week, but later he let on that he considered it a great joke.

While he was away, Fanny supervised a small army of gardeners. She also went to endless parties and receptions at the grand houses in the neighbourhood, driving in horse-drawn carriages and often taking the boys, much against their will. To Raoul, all these functions seemed exactly the same: at every one the White or the Blue Hungarian band would be playing Strauss waltzes and martial airs in park or garden, and the only interest for him was the astonishing tightness of the musicians' uniforms. The conductor of one orchestra, enormously fat and rubicund, once asked Fanny if her son was exceptionally musical, as he had noticed the boy gazing at his players with rapt attention. In fact Raoul was hypnotised by the tension of their gold-frogged uniforms, and longing for the explosion which he felt sure must come.

Sometimes Fanny took the children to stay in other large country houses, and to Raoul none seemed more palatial than Patshull, near Wolverhampton. As a footman escorted the boy to his room in a corner of the vast building, he said, 'Breakfast is at 8.30, Sir, and his Lordship would like you to play golf with him at 10 a.m. I beg of you to allow him to win, otherwise our lives will not be worth living.' Next morning, as their host hacked his way round the private nine-hole course, spraying divots down the fairway, Raoul began to understand the footman's anxiety. The noble lord became ever more purple in the face with frustration, but he won by one hole, and afterwards he said to Fanny, 'What a nice boy you've got! Do bring him again.'

At home, between parties, Fanny did her best to bring up her children. She felt it her duty to take them to church on Sundays, as well as at Christmas and Easter, but the services bored them rigid, and had the opposite effect to that intended. They could hardly fail to notice that their mother's religious enthusiasm waxed or waned according to her degree of friendship with the vicar, and Raoul grew up a robust atheist, distressed by the way in which rival religions fight each other.

CHAPTER TWO

UNWILLINGLY TO SCHOOL

Before he was eight years old, Raoul was sent off to St Edmund's at Grayshott, a preparatory school which he immediately hated. Nobody had warned him that, because of financial difficulties, the school had just been obliged to amalgamate with another, which contained a high proportion of young thugs. All Raoul knew was that on his first day he was tied to a tree and repeatedly shot from close range with a catapult. He also had carbolic soap forced into his mouth, and was made to swallow it. Two other new boys, from more sheltered backgrounds, could not stand such treatment and bolted for home on the first night. The staff must have realised that something was wrong and after Raoul had been nearly drowned in the swimming pool, being held under water by four senior boys until he passed out, they at last took action. The thugs disappeared, but the incident left Raoul with an ineradicable fear of being under water.

Gradually he learned to fend for himself, helped by the fact that, when he was nine, a friend of his father, who had been a champion amateur boxer, taught him the rudiments of self-defence. As this mentor had worked for years on a ranch in the United States, he was also a dead-eye revolver shot, and imparted many useful skills.

St Edmund's had good playing fields and a short golf course, but Raoul soon realised that he lacked the competitive instinct needed for team games, or even for the more individual athletics. His only major success was in the long jump, at which his 'extended undercarriage' gave him an advantage. (When he was about nine, his mother took him to see the great Nijinsky dance at Covent Garden. As they emerged from the theatre, she said, 'What did you think of that? Wasn't it marvellous?' To which he is alleged to have replied: 'He'd certainly beat Stokes Major in the high jump.')

He played cricket, soccer and rugger for the school 'in an undistinguished way', making a few runs and scoring the odd goal or try. It was characteristic of the Spartan regime that boys considered it sissy to wear pads when batting. He also 'just managed to scrape through exams'. He was more interested in wildlife, and

kept several lizards and a white rat called Charlie in his pocket.

The middle of one term was enlivened by a thrilling adventure. Some of the boys went off for their half-term weekend in horse-drawn brakes, and Raoul was allowed to take the reins of his. All went well until they reached the Devil's Punchbowl, the steep hill near Hindhead then still crowned by the gallows from which the last highwayman was reputed to have been hung. At the top of the hill the old coachman cautioned Raoul to take it easy, and reminded him that there was a sharp bend at the bottom: 'The slower the better, boy!'

Just as they came down to the corner, an enormous open Mercedes roared round the bend, with two red-faced men in the bucket seats and a bonnet which 'seemed to go on for ever'. The howl of the engine, the explosions from the exhaust and the crash of gears as the driver changed down for the hill – all this sudden commotion terrified the horses, which bolted. The next second the carriage was hurtling downhill, out of control and rocking wildly from side to side. Neither brake nor reins had the slightest effect. The coachman began yelling '*Whoa!*', his voice high with alarm, but the boys in the back, not realising what danger they were in, shouted, 'Good old Millais! Let 'em rip!'

By sheer luck the vehicle negotiated the bend on two wheels, then crashed back onto four and kept going. At last, to his unspeakable relief, Raoul found they were on an uphill gradient, and with the coachman's help he managed to pull the horses to a halt, sweat pouring from them. He, too, was perspiring with fear and effort, and for a few seconds he sat in a daze, vaguely aware of a tumult of congratulations coming from behind him. Belatedly he realised that he was being hailed as a hero – 'an unaccustomed experience', and one which he had the sense not to spoil by revealing that it was luck rather than skill or effort on his part which had saved them all from a horrible smash.

When he was twelve, the school took on a new master, a fine-looking man and a former captain in the army. Having been an instructor on military ranges, he started a shooting club and taught

Raoul, here seen at Bisley, on the right of the middle row in the St Edmund's Eight of 1914, did not much care for his preparatory school at Grayshott, but found that rifle-shooting was one sport at which he could excel.

the boys to fire .22 rifles. Raoul found his *métier*. Here was a sport at which he could shine. In the summer of 1914 he won the Donegal Medal with a score of 203 out of 210 – and so good was the new master's coaching that at Michaelmas 1914, within a year of his arrival, the school VIII went to Bisley and won the St George's Shield, competed for by all the prep schools in England. A fine photograph survives, showing the VIII in smart tweed knickerbocker suits with stiff white Eton collars sitting uncomfortably high outside the necks of their jackets.

After a triumphant return to St Edmund's, the captain initiated a school competition, and persuaded one of the governors,

General Wodehouse, to present a prize. For this – a magnificent Greener match rifle, with gold engraving and special sights – Raoul conceived a powerful longing, and he spent every spare moment practising. Alas, the competition was decided on handicap, and although he excelled himself by scoring 298 out of 300, he was beaten by a boy whose handicap of 120 gave him a score of 302. Looking back, Raoul remembered feeling that the bottom had dropped out of his world, but that the captain was even more upset.

It was this same master who rescued Raoul from academic oblivion. Somehow he instilled in him such an interest in Latin and Greek, and taught the languages so well, that the headmaster decided he was a potential classical scholar, and sent him to sit the entrance exam at that most academically exacting of public schools, Winchester. There he obtained 98 per cent in Greek, over

80 per cent in Latin and two per cent in mathematics – a result which astounded the college authorities but nevertheless secured him a place.

Raoul later regarded his father's decision to send him to Winchester as 'a grave mistake.' He was a born nonconformist, and although he did not exactly fight against discipline, from the moment of his arrival at public school he had the sensation of being a square peg in an establishment where all the holes, designed for the production of scholarly recruits for the Foreign Office and the Civil Service, were perfectly round.

In the autumn of 1915 he found himself at Cook's (also known as Du Boulay's), a brick-and-flint Victorian boys' boarding house. He was tall for his age, long-legged and almost painfully thin. His first task was to learn the archaic argot of the school: 'half' for 'term', 'man' for 'boy', 'pitch up' for 'parents', 'tother' for 'prep school' and so on, and his initiation was no less painful than that at St Edmund's.

The six prefects in each house enjoyed the privilege of beating as many of the junior men as they liked, and Raoul, being the only new man that half, was flogged ten times during his first fortnight, for no discernible reason. The final straw came when he was thrashed in his gallery (dormitory) by 'a short-sighted but sadistic brute called Ashton'. The weapon used was an officer's swagger-stick tipped with a steel ferrule, which was strictly illegal, as only an ash switch was permitted, and since the victim was wearing only thin pyjamas, his agony can be imagined. He managed not to scream, but after six strokes, given with a gloating pause between each, blood was running down his legs, and the spectacle became too much for the other boys, who were watching silently from their beds. Suddenly they broke ranks, rushed at the bully, knocked off his spectacles and bore him to the floor.

A few days later the tall, fat and flabby senior prefect, who considered himself a sharp dresser and always carried a rolled umbrella, came into Cook's mugging hall – the large room with cubicles known as toys round the sides, where the boys kept their belongings and did their preparation for the following day. Sauntering along the hall, the prefect stopped opposite Raoul's toy, and, when the boy did not look up, began to prod him in the ribs

By nature a loner, Raoul resented discipline from an early age, and spent much of his boyhood roaming the country fields near his home in Sussex, augmenting his pocket money by the sale of rabbits which he ferreted and shot.

with the point of his umbrella.

Eighty years on, Raoul has not forgotten how the iron entered into his soul. 'This is enough,' he thought. 'I've nothing to lose. Here goes.' Rising slowly to his feet, he swung his right fist and hit the prefect on the point of the chin. The older boy went down as if poleaxed. There was a moment's stunned silence, then the whole room rose up and let out a roar. When Raoul kicked the hated umbrella across the floor, it was somehow spirited away and never seen again.

'Christ, Millais!' muttered the prefect. 'I'll get you for this!' Although four years older, he lacked the guts to retaliate, and made his unsteady way to the door amid a barrage of catcalls. Raoul supposed that his career at Winchester was finished, but far from it: no prefect ever bothered him again.

In class, however, he could not find his feet. Because he had scored so well in the entrance exam, he was placed in a higher division than he could cope with, alongside boys two years older, and he never came to terms with the teaching. After a year or so he gave up the struggle and devoted himself to the more important business of supplementing the boys' meagre rations.

In wartime, with food rationed, it was obviously hard for their elderly bachelor housemaster, Murray Hicks, to feed thirty-odd ravenous boys. (They referred to him as 'the Tec', from his habit of creeping about the passages in felt slippers after lights out.) But that was no excuse for the repulsive nature of the meals served up by the cook, Mrs Bonetti. The boys put it about that her ancestors must have been employed by the Borgias, as many of her young victims ended up in the school sanatorium with acute stomach pains. Lunch often consisted of 'strips of ancient shoe leather, a hard potato and slug salad'; a prize was given each week to the boy who found the maximum number of foreign bodies in his portion.

One day a large hunk of salt pork was seen to be covered in dead bluebottles. Having inspected it with revulsion, the boys returned to their places and banged their spoons on the tables, shouting. '*Poison! Poison!*' The Tec came in, surveyed the offensive joint and had it removed – but its replacement was 'something that closely resembled cricket-boot soles with the studs left in'.

After that demonstration things improved slightly, and the better-off boys could supplement their official meals by buying treats like eggs and sausage and mash from the school shop. But many of them were too poor for such extravagances, and hunger drove Raoul to make his own arrangements.

At the beginning of the next half he brought with him a short-barrelled .22 rifle which broke down into two pieces. With this he set off for marauding expeditions on his bogle (bicycle), the barrel lodged in the clips designed for the pump, underneath the cross-bar, and the stock slung on a strap over his shoulder inside his jacket. As soon as lunch was over he would pedal off, either northwards through the town (which was strictly forbidden) or southwards towards St Cross, then a village a mile out in the country, often carrying a fishing rod as well.

There an old lady, a friend of his mother's, gave him permission to fish on her beat of the River Itchen, on the understanding that he would remove as many pike and cannibal trout as he could from her stretch of the water – a challenge which suited him ideally. Using the two lower sections of an 18-foot greenheart salmon rod handed down from his grandfather, he attached a rabbit snare to the leading end and stalked his prey like a human otter.

Whenever he spotted a worthwhile target lying deep below one of the banks, he would slip into the water downstream and make a cautious approach, waist- or even neck-deep. His method was to slip his noose round the tail of the fish and move it very slowly on towards the head; when the snare reached the gills, he would make a sudden thrust, upwards and forwards. If his aim and timing were right, he would land the fish on the bank. By this means he cleared most of the predatory monsters from his beat, and thereafter enjoyed good fly-fishing. On many an evening in summer he returned to base with the pockets of his mackintosh full of trout, which, with the help of Mr Court, the house butler, he and his friends cooked over their single gas ring.

The boys benefited still more from his shooting expeditions, conducted on land belonging to friendly farmers on either side of the river. One winter day, with snow lying deep on the ground, he was bicycling slowly along a lane when he spotted a covey of partridges sheltering against the foot of a haystack. He rode on for a few yards, left the bicycle in a ditch and crept back. He peered through a gap in the hedge and saw the birds huddled less than 30 yards away. Taking careful aim with his .22, he shot the left-hand one. When it rolled over fluttering, the others, to his amazement, paid little attention. Maybe they were stupefied by the cold: in any case, he picked off all eight, one after the other, and returned laden to Cook's, where about twenty boys tucked in to a sumptuous feast.

After this triumph, competition to accompany Raoul became strong, but he always resisted it and continued to go out alone, because he knew that if he were caught, he would almost certainly be expelled, and he did not want anyone else to suffer. This prohibition extended even to his closest friend, the agreeably eccentric seventh Marquess of Waterford, commonly known as 'Whisky Waterford', who once hid Raoul's braces just as they were due to go on an Officers' Training Corps parade. On another occasion, after some trivial row, several boys were standing in the courtyard when they heard a shout. Looking up, they saw Whisky about to drop a basin of water on them from the third floor – a move which might easily have proved fatal.

On the playing fields, as in the classroom, Raoul suffered (or benefited) from his lack of competitive instinct. Nature had endowed him with no desire to outdo his fellows, and not even the fact that D.R. Jardine – captain of the England Cricket XI during the bodyline crisis of 1933 – was in his house could fire him with enthusiasm for games.

In school, he somehow managed to bump along, with many narrow escapes. On one occasion, in chapel, the lining of a pocket containing his catapult ammunition gave way, releasing a carpet of swan-shot, like small ball-bearings, onto the floor of the aisle. Chaos ensued; it was as if the marble tiles had been covered with banana skins, and the scholars went down by the dozen as they trooped out. Luckily Raoul kept his head, managed not to turn round to see what was happening, and thus escaped detection.

Another uncomfortable experience reinforced his conviction that he was 'the wrong man in the wrong place'. One night in 1916, as searchlight beams flickered about the sky, they picked up a Zeppelin, and the boys all rushed to the windows of their dormitory to watch the invader. The housemaster appeared and ordered everyone into the basement, as if the school had been designated the enemy's target for the night. When his order was greeted with derisive laughter, he took names and threatened delinquents with birchings by the headmaster. Next day Raoul and Whisky Waterford were sent for and accused of being the ringleaders who had incited others to mutiny. In fact 90 per cent of the boys had ignored the Tec's order spontaneously, and Raoul felt that he was once again being singled out as unacceptable Wykehamist material.

So his school career sputtered on; but his third year at Winchester was clouded by a family tragedy. At the start of the Great War his brother Geoff – 'the only character I have come across who was born genuinely unafraid of any man or anything' – had run away from Repton, aged seventeen, and enlisted as a trooper in the Sussex Yeomanry. Many of the officers had known him in peacetime, and the commanding officer came to see Johnny Millais, telling him that his son would be wasted as a groom and should get a commission. Johnny wrote to his old friend the Duke of Bedford, who was in the process of re-forming the Bedfordshire Regiment and raising a battalion; as a result Geoff was commissioned a junior second lieutenant, and reported to Woburn

Although Raoul hated Winchester, and left the school prematurely, just before he was expelled, he looks relatively cheerful in this house group of 1916 (third from left, back row), with his arms folded and – no doubt – a catapult in his pocket.

without revealing that he was under age.

The old duke and duchess – she was nearly stone deaf – took a fancy to him, and he began to spend every off-duty weekend at Woburn Abbey. The duchess was a keen shot, and on Saturdays gamekeepers and estate workers would drive clouds of pheasants and partridges over the pair of them. No one else was invited to shoot, and the cartridges were free.

Whenever Geoff came home on leave, he would tell wonderful stories of his adventures; but then drafts from the regiment began to be sent to the trenches in France, and he refused to be left behind. Many years after the war, Raoul came on a letter which

the old duke had written to his father:

Dear Johnny,

I have some disturbing news about Geoff. As you know, we are devoted to him, and look upon him almost as our son. But he's a very headstrong boy, and yesterday he came to see me. He was obviously in a state of great agitation. He said that if he was left behind again when the next draft went to France, he would desert. I know he's under age, but what can I do? I'm convinced he'll do what he says.

So Geoff went into battle, and soon he established a reputation for reckless courage. A sergeant who knew him in the trenches told the family, after the war, that Geoff was the finest officer he had ever served with. Not only would the men follow him everywhere; whenever food was short, he gave away his own rations. At the front, his favourite pastime was to creep out into no-man's land during the night, armed with a couple of grenades and a pick-axe handle, and crawl up on any enemy machine-gun nest which had been giving trouble. Choosing his moment, when he hoped the occupants were asleep, he would lob a couple of grenades and then jump in himself to finish off any survivors. In this way, the sergeant reckoned, Geoff must have killed more Germans single-handed than any other infantryman during the war.

His luck held out until three days before the Armistice of 11 November 1918. Then, for the last time, he went over the top, with a pick-axe handle in one hand and a captured German Luger in the other. A machine-gun bullet took him in the chest. He was carried off on a stretcher, but died of wounds next day, and was buried in the military cemetery at Sailly-au-Bois.

Geoff's death was a grievous blow to all the family, but especially to Raoul, then just seventeen and still struggling to come to terms with the alien environment of Winchester. The loss of his beloved brother and mentor finally undermined his attempts to toe the academic line.

At the start of the Easter half in 1919 he was sent for by the housemaster, who said he intended to make him a prefect. Raoul declined the honour, and when asked why, revealed what had happened during his first few days in the school. The Tec seemed astounded, and said, 'Why on earth didn't you tell me?' The public-school ethics of those days of course made any such sneaking impossible.

For the whole of that half Raoul cut science lessons; but because he always arranged for someone to answer his name at roll-call, his absence went unnoticed until end-of-half examinations revealed a suspicious blank opposite the name of Millais. He was sent for by the Tec. He found the housemaster in a rage, and, because he assumed he would be leaving the school for ever on the first train next morning, he made a clean breast of all the illegal fishing and shooting that had taken the place of his scientific education.

His confession did nothing to improve the Tec's temper. On the contrary, the housemaster was incensed by the implication that he had been starving his boys for years, and further infuriated by the discovery that Raoul had consistently broken school rules without being caught. 'I shall send you to the headmaster immediately!' he roared.

So Raoul found himself standing at one end of a long refectory table in the headmaster's study, waiting for the great M.J. Rendall to appear. In those anxious moments he remembered with some disquiet the occasion on which, with his catapult, he had shot two of the head man's Rhode Island red hens out of the French division window, which was directly above the run in the back yard, and the great difficulty he had had in retrieving them.

Suddenly, from behind a dark curtain, out he came – a tall man with a thick brown moustache which, to Raoul, made him look 'as though he was retrieving a large rat'. One of his minor failings was that he pretended to know every boy in the school, and so could never ask anyone what he was called. (Equally, it was a matter of principle that boys never gave their names.) Now, having drawn himself up to his full height, with hands on lapels, he launched off in characteristic fashion: 'Ah now, Miller.'

'My name's not Miller, Sir.'

'Ah no, of course. You're Milner.'

'No, Sir.'

'Well, Mills, then.'

'No, Sir.'

'Not *Millais*, surely?'

'Yes, Sir.'

'Oh yes – of course.'

With that little matter cleared up, he began to read out a list of the miscreant's shortcomings, ending up with a tirade which Raoul remembered for ever after verbatim. 'You're unquestionably the worst man I have ever had under my jurisdiction in this school. I have heard from your housemaster the full story of your illegal activities, and now the unforgivable fact that during the whole half you failed to attend science lectures. It is therefore my duty to birch you. Have you anything to say?'

'Yes, Sir,' replied Raoul. 'I'm leaving for good on the first train tomorrow.' And with a flash of inspiration he added, 'Wouldn't it be a pity if I left here with a bad impression at both ends?'

For a few seconds the headmaster appeared to be stunned. Then he pulled himself together and shouted, 'That's the most impertinent remark I have ever had the misfortune to have addressed to me! You are clearly incorrigible.'

With that he vanished behind the curtain. Raoul, assuming that he was about to be flogged, decided to make a bolt for it, and was on the point of doing so when the head popped out into view again.

'I've given the matter careful thought, Miller,' he said. 'Owing to the fact that times have been hard, and that you may have lacked parental discipline during your father's absences abroad, I am prepared to overlook your insubordinate behaviour. Nevertheless, I feel that the college will benefit greatly from your absence. Goodbye.'

Exit Millais, at the double, clutching straw hat.

Back at home, when Raoul revealed what had happened, he thought his father was going to have a stroke, so inordinately did he laugh. Johnny hated schoolmasters, having had the same sort of trouble at Marlborough, so he merely remarked that history had repeated itself, and passed no censure. But when Raoul said, 'I got away with it, didn't I?' he was told that on no account must he be smug: he might not always be so lucky.

Raoul's drawing of his younger sister Rosamund, two years
his junior. Because she took up much of their nanny's time
when they were young, Raoul often found himself locked
into an attic box room, with strict instructions to keep still.

CHAPTER THREE

YOUNG MAN ABOUT TOWN

In the drawings done on the walls of his attic prison at Compton's Brow, and far more in pictures of flowers painted at Winchester, Raoul had already demonstrated some of the artistic precocity shown by his grandfather. His formal training began in 1920, when he went to the Byam Shaw School of Art in Notting Hill Gate. At first he commuted from Horsham to London, taking his motorcycle on the train and riding it about the capital, where he had frequent accidents, once sliding under a bus in Piccadilly but emerging unscathed.

At art school he began like all the students, bored to tears by the drudgery of drawing marble busts – the traditional initiation, but after a couple of months liberation arrived in the form of a teacher called Ernest Jackson, who was not only an inspired instructor but also a fervent admirer of Raoul's grandfather. Perhaps this made him take extra trouble over the latest Millais scion; at any rate, Raoul learned a great deal from him, and has remained indebted to him ever since.

One day, to his dismay, he found a model from the life class crying in a corner during a rest period. The girl had a severe squint and Raoul, feeling sorry for her, took her out to lunch. She was twenty-six, and to him, 'a callow nineteen', she poured out a tale of woe, telling him how her whole life had been blighted by her disability. The incident made a lasting impression on Raoul; never before had he seen anyone in such distress, and he felt inadequate at not being able to help.

As his skill grew, his father at last began to take more interest in him, renting a studio for him in Church Street, Kensington, and giving him an allowance. This was enough for Raoul to enjoy himself in London, especially as Ferrari, the Mâitre d'Hotel at the Berkeley, in Berkeley Square, was extremely generous to students. If someone took a girl to dinner there, Ferrari would charge them £5 and never present a bill. (Raoul was enraged when this most ardent of Anglophiles was interned on the Isle of Man during the Second World War and treated as a potential spy.)

Another favourite resort was the Four Hundred Club in Leicester Square, of which Raoul was a founder member, and where Leo, the manager, knew the intimate details of every member's private life: 'Lord B. was asking after you last week, Sir. Unfortunately he's having a short spell in the clinic.' Members brought along their own bottles of brandy, whisky or gin, and even if someone had not been to the club for a year, his own bottle, with his name on the label, would be on the table to greet him. The dance music was played by Tim Clayton and his quintet. He, too, knew his customers: whenever Raoul appeared, he would launch into his favourite tune of the moment, 'Riding High'.

In the holidays Raoul often stayed with his godfather, Archie Thorburn, and spent hours watching the great bird artist at work in his studio. But as Thorburn always painted in watercolours and Raoul never did, the young man did not learn as much as he might have. A more productive visit was to the animal painter Frank Calderon, RA, and his fiery wife Ethel, who lived in Kent. On the day after Raoul's arrival she launched a dinner plate at her husband's head, and when Raoul threatened to report her for assault, they became firm friends. Calderon proved a forthright teacher. 'If you don't know what's inside an animal, you can't paint what's outside,' he told Raoul; and, to the young man's disgust, he took him to an abattoir, where he made him cut up a dead horse.

That same year, 1920, Raoul was elected a member of the Garrick Club, which then had the reputation of providing the best food in London. On his inaugural visit he was welcomed by his two heavyweight backers, Sir Edwin Lutyens, architect of New Delhi, and Gerald du Maurier, the celebrated actor. During a guided tour of the building they showed him a large self-portrait of his grandfather hanging over a mantelpiece upstairs, and told him that J.E., together with his friend Sir John Hare, had resuscitated the club during the last century.

As they came down the main staircase, Raoul noticed a distinguished-looking man poised before the umbrella stand in the hall, with his back to them. 'That's old Sir Squire Bancroft having a pee,' du Maurier confided. 'Take no notice of him – but never leave your umbrella there before lunch, my boy.' Lutyens spent much of the meal drawing fantastical designs on the tablecloth and giving their young guest running commentaries on the members lunching there that day: 'That's a famous KC, biggest bore in London . . . That man sitting alone in the corner writes wonderfully amusing children's books. Never go near him: he's got no sense of humour whatever . . . That's an actor who thinks he's Sir Henry Irving . . .'

Raoul soon realised that he was at least fifteen years younger than most of the members, and sixty years younger than some. But as he was based in London, and at art school five days a week, he frequently lunched and dined at the Garrick, being accepted 'as a gauche stripling with perhaps an acceptable background'.

On Wednesday afternoons he would often repair to the Coliseum, in St Martin's Lane, where music hall was flourishing. In those days, before the formation of the Crazy Gang, Flanagan and Allen, Nervo and Knox and Naughton and Gold all did separate double acts, backed up by individuals like Max Miller (the Cheeky Chappie), Grock, the great French clown, and the Tramp Cyclist. The point about all these turns was that they never varied: like three quarters of the audience, Raoul always knew exactly what was coming, and he took immense delight in recognising every gag.

One of his favourites was Grock who, having played the piano in enormous white gloves, would unpack an outsize trunk and bring out mounds of underpants, ties, socks and other clothes. Then from the very bottom he would produce a violin 6in long, which he would proceed to play beautifully, still wearing his gloves.

The Tramp always rode out of the wings on his bicycle, clad in black garments so voluminous that they trailed along the floor. After a couple of circuits he threw away his handlebars and continued on the back wheel. Then he began to scratch, clearly troubled by vermin about his person. Having dismounted, he produced an old box mousetrap from his clothes and with a knowing leer returned it to the inner recesses of his suit. Soon there would come a loud snap of the trap-door closing, and with a blissful expression the Tramp would present the audience with evidence of his success. He would then draw a .45 revolver from his sleeve, and, with a terrific explosion, shoot his victim through the bars of the little cage – a performance which invariably brought the house down.

In 1919 Raoul had acquired an AV Monocar, a single-seater, shaped like a red bullet, with the engine sitting up behind the driver's head, open to the elements. The only method of starting was to push the vehicle downhill, running beside it until the engine fired, and then leaping aboard. The transmission consisted of a rubber belt, which frequently broke, and as this also controlled

the steering, progress was erratic to say the least.

The AV was the first in a long succession of motor vehicles. Three-quarters of a century later, Raoul confesses that he has 'always been hypnotised' by the design and performance of cars: chain-driven Mercedes, Bentleys, ACs, Facel Vegas, Buicks, Chryslers, Delages, Dodges, Broughs, Fiats, Jensens (three), Jaguars (six, including the first Swallow), Lloyd Lords, Fords, Borgwards, Isotta-Fraschinis, Seats, Subarus (four), he has had them all, and for more than seventy-five years he kept his driving licence clean. In the early days he perforce became expert at doing his own servicing, and whenever he went on a long journey – for instance to Scotland – he carried spare cans of petrol, as there were few garages along the road.

In 1921 he went on from the Byam Shaw to the Royal Academy Schools, to which he made a typically unorthodox entry. Instead of submitting several life drawings, a landscape and a still life as requested, he put in fifty drawings of animals. When the committee sent for him, one of them asked, 'Why didn't you let us have what we asked for?' Raoul replied, 'I thought you wanted to see if I could draw', whereupon 'two ancient greybeards began to shake with laughter', and one said to the other, 'He's as bad as his grandfather – insubordinate as anything. We'd better let him in.'

At the Academy Schools Raoul made a lifelong friend in the form of Laurence Irving, grandson of the great actor Sir Henry Irving, and son of H.B. Irving, the actor-manager. Laurence had been a fighter pilot during the First World War, and now invited Raoul to lodge with his family in the Crescent, in Regent's Park. Laurence's father was dead, but his mother had also been on the stage under her maiden name, Dorothea Baird, and the Irving household was always full of actors and actresses dropping in for meals. To Raoul, Dorothea became Aunt Dolly, and a second mother.

Living in Regent's Park, he was within easy walking distance of London Zoo, and he made frequent visits, drawing the animals on two days every week. Fascinated though he was by wild creatures, he hated to see big cats and eagles imprisoned in lifelong confinement, and he befriended a Bengal tiger called Rajah. Arriving early, before any other visitors, he would spend hours watching the tiger pad up and down his dark cell.

After a while the animal came to recognise him, and whenever Raoul appeared he would jump up and rub himself, purring, against the bars of the cage. One day, when no other humans were about, Raoul vaulted the barrier and, when the tiger lay down, put a hand through the bars to scratch him behind the ears. This intimacy lasted several weeks, until the officious keeper suddenly appeared and reported Raoul to the authorities, who banned him from the zoo. Two years later he once again crept into the Lion House. Rajah was asleep, but when Raoul called to him, he leapt up, came to the bars and began to purr. The little saga left Raoul

21

with mixed emotions: he knew he had been foolish to court danger so recklessly, yet at the same time he felt he was the only friend the tiger had ever known.

One result of his zoo-going was an extraordinary painting of a lion attacking a white horse – a work which, if it owes a good deal to Stubbs, is nevertheless an amazingly accomplished and powerful piece of work for a twenty-one-year-old.

The professional artists who came into the Royal Academy Schools as visiting instructors, supposedly to encourage the students and to impart artistic knowledge, tended to be amateurish in their approach to teaching. Although they were friendly, they seemed shy, and anxious to get through the morning or afternoon as quickly as possible. There was one, however, who was neither agreeable nor self-effacing: the horse artist, A.J. Munnings, who first exhibited at the Academy in 1898, became an Academician in 1924, and was President from 1944 to 1951. For him Raoul conceived a lifelong dislike amounting to enmity. He acknowledged Munnings' enormous talent and commercial success, but could not stand him as a person, finding him brash, bombastic and horribly jealous of any other artist who seemed to threaten his supremacy. When, as a twenty-year-old student, Raoul asked him what he thought of that other excellent horse artist Lionel Edwards, Munnings replied dismissively, 'Rotten painter. Quite a good illustrator.'

Raoul never forgave him for that insulting dismissal – and his dislike was well reciprocated. When Munnings became President of the Royal Academy during the Second World War, he let it be known that if Raoul ever submitted any pictures for the Summer Exhibition, he personally would make sure that none was accepted. In reply Raoul sent a message saying, 'I take this as a great compliment' – and he was gratified to hear that Munnings flew into a rage. The long-term result of this mutual hostility was that Raoul steered clear of the Academy all his life, made deprecating references to it, and finished many letters to friends with the ironic 'Failed RA' in brackets after his signature.

His favourite visiting teacher by far was Augustus John, another devoted admirer of his grandfather. John was then in his early forties, but already a confirmed alcoholic. Poking his head round the door of the life class in the evening, he would lurch unsteadily forward, slump down next to Raoul and fall asleep with his head on the student's shoulder. If, after a while, Raoul offered him his charcoal stick and said, 'Please, show me how to do it,' he would mutter, 'Very good, my boy. Keep going' and nod off again. When John took a box at the Chelsea Arts Ball, he invited Raoul as a guest, and they spent most of the night pouring champagne on the dancers.

So, for a while, Raoul became a man about town. But his heart was still in the country, and he became a connoisseur of hunt balls. Wherever they took place, the same gang of his friends seemed to congregate, and whenever they danced the night away, they were fuelled largely by high spirits: there was little drinking, practically no sex, and certainly no question of drugs. For Raoul, one highlight was always the arrival of kedgeree at 3 a.m.

At home in Sussex, he and a friend formed a pack of liver-coloured Sussex spaniels, eight couple strong. These little dogs, which he described as 'comical, short-legged harriers', hunted to a horn, and were soon in strong demand as beaters on rabbit shoots. They seemed to have an inbuilt instinct to spread out as they entered a covert, and their low stature enabled them to hunt under any brambles; moreover, in spite of their noisy excitement, they remained easy to control. Raoul ferried them about in an ancient pick-up truck with a canvas hood, and sometimes even took them to Scotland.

Already, at the age of twenty, he had strong views on the idiocy of much modern art. What he called 'the Picasso lark' had just started, and for a joke, he submitted a painting of a horse and cart in a city street at the Royal Academy Schools. The horse had one eye in the middle of its forehead; the cart had square wheels, and the driver 'needed an ambulance.' Of course, the picture was highly commended.

OPPOSITE:
Lion attacking horse. This apocalyptic painting, done when Raoul was twenty-one, perhaps owed something to his frequent visits to Regent's Park Zoo, where he felt sorry for the solitary big cats, and befriended a tiger called Rajah.

Neptune arises from the waves on the certificate awarded to Raoul to show he had crossed the Equator aboard the German ship *Usaramo*, on the way to his second African safari, in 1925. He was outraged by the corruption prevailing in the Portuguese colony of Angola.

CHAPTER FOUR

AFRICA

Then, as now, the timing of courses at the Royal Academy Schools was exceedingly relaxed. Students could come and go as they liked, and at the end of 1923 Raoul broke away on the first great adventure of his life, to accompany his father on a big-game safari in the southern Sudan. He was twenty-two years old, 6ft 4in tall, slender but strong, and went equipped not only with sketching materials but also with two German mouth-organs which he bought in the port at Southampton.

His father was then fifty-eight. As usual he had been working all out, and he had decided to take an extended holiday, mounting the expedition with Raoul as his sole companion. The two embarked on the *City of Canterbury*, a small cargo vessel, on 1 December, and as the ship pottered along the Mediterranean, through the Suez Canal and down the Red Sea, Raoul made dozens of sketches, backed up by notes, which he later worked up into finished drawings. One notable success was his picture of a fighting Arab horseman whom he saw at a demonstration laid on for the benefit of tourists in Algiers.

Among the few passengers was one Major Maydon, exactly the type who had often appeared at Compton's Brow when Raoul was a boy: a former army officer, a nomad who had travelled to the ends of the empire and come back brimming with stories of far-flung places. This wanderer was a gifted natural linguist who learned by ear and spoke four or five languages fluently. Now for a fortnight he gave Raoul an hour's instruction a day in basic Arabic.

After fifteen days the ship docked at Port Sudan, on the shore of the Red Sea. The country for which the party was aiming lay far to the south, but as a warm-up they hired servants and set off westwards across the Red Sea Desert on camels to hunt ibex in the Buwatti mountains. Raoul, to whom every facet of Africa was

Fighting Arab on horseback, sketched by Raoul after a demonstration laid on for tourists in Algiers. His first trip to Africa, made with his father in 1923-24, revealed his enormous talent at line drawing.

After several narrow escapes big-game hunting with his father west of the Nile, Raoul decided that buffaloes, with their tremendous weight, strength and speed over a short distance, were the most dangerous of all large animals.

new and thrilling, was allotted a white thoroughbred racer, which he named George – a splendid animal whose only serious drawback was a tendency to whip round and launch vicious bites at his rider. Rumour had it that George, earlier the pride of the Sudanese Camel Corps, had severely damaged his former rider when he seized him by the nape of the neck and almost bit his head off – whereupon he had been cashiered. Once in motion, however, he was fast and tireless, with a gait far more comfortable than the lurching swagger of the baggage animals.

The inhabitants of the area were the Hadendowa tribe, wild, brave, warlike people, known to the British as 'fuzzy-wuzzies' from their wiry hair, and famous for having broken the enemy square at the battle of Omdurman in 1898. They seemed delighted to receive white visitors, and were glad to take them hunting; but

once the party reached the mountains, Raoul found conditions extremely testing. Having no head for heights, he suffered from vertigo as they crept at dawn along narrow paths, with precipitous rock faces plunging sheer away into the mist below. Once he was faced by the unnerving phenomenon known as the Spectre of the Brocken in which, with the sunrise behind him, he was confronted by his own gigantic shadow projected onto a white wall of haze ahead, so that a colossal figure seemed to be advancing on him with menace and determination.

Johnny would have preferred to stalk the ibex, but Ali Mahommed, sheikh of the Buwatti Hadendowas, insisted on organising immense drives, with up to eighty beaters converging along the mountain tracks from miles around, and the two riflemen posted on separate vantage points. Between them they shot several good ibex, which increased their standing among the natives. Yet, carnivorous though they were, the Hadendowas would not eat ibex meat. Instead, they invited the white men to a ceremonial feast of goat, offering them the eyes on the ends of slivers of horn. By sleight of hand the guests managed to secrete these treasures in their trouser pockets, but the main course, described by Raoul as 'army issue boots with the laces intact', was hardly more palatable, and he decided that 'Capricorn has never been my favourite star'.

Fortified by this fierce inauguration, the hunters took the train to Khartoum, where Johnny's renown as hunter-naturalist ensured that they were treated as very important persons. They were met by an old friend, Captain Courtney Brocklehurst, Chief Game Warden of the country, known as Brock, who drove them to Government House – a white marble palace built by Kitchener – to stay with the Sirdar, or Governor, Sir Lee Stack. To his alarm, Raoul found the place full of grandees in tail- or frock-coats, most notably Prince Arthur of Connaught (Queen Victoria's third son), together with his wife.

Early one morning Brock took Raoul to the zoo to see a fine lion called Sayed. The animal appeared to be exceptionally docile and benevolent, and lay on its back waving its legs in the air while they scratched its stomach; but when Raoul told his father about

the incident, he was furious. 'Never do that again,' he said. 'One day he won't be feeling so good, and there'll be an accident.'

As the ancient paddle steam *Omdurman* bore the hunters up the Nile, the land, the animals and above all the birds seized Raoul's imagination. Here were any number of species he had never seen before: spoonbills, black storks, sand grouse, glossy ibis and the glorious Abyssinian roller, known locally as 'the Oxford and Cambridge bird' from its dark and light blue plumage.

When the boat tied up on the bank to load wood for fuel, Raoul took his shotgun and Mahommed, their 'slightly treacherous cook', on a walk upstream, to see if he could supplement the normal menu, which had already featured young crocodile, iguana and cat. When two white-faced ducks flew past, he dropped both

Ali Mahommed, Sheikh of the Hadendowa tribe, gives out his orders for an immense ibex drive in the Buwatti Mountains, west of the Red Sea Desert. On the precipitous, rocky tracks and ledges, Raoul found himself troubled by vertigo.

'*Effendi*,' replied Mahommed scornfully, 'no crocs north of Malakal.'

With that he plunged into the water. He collected both ducks and was returning in triumph when out of the reeds along the bank burst a 15ft grey torpedo. Reloading instantly, Raoul gave it two barrels, which diverted the croc from its intended victim, but when Mahommed reached the bank he lay there for a long time in a state of shock and exhaustion. He told the party that Raoul had saved his life, but Raoul later realised that the opposite was true. He should not have let Mahommed enter the water at all; his youth and lack of experience had almost thrown the man's life away.

One night as they steamed upriver a dug-out canoe drew alongside. The sole occupant, a young white man, came aboard and asked for Raoul's father, whom he knew, and the two had a joyful reunion. He was the younger son of an aristocratic English family who had opted out and for the past ten years had lived up and down the Nile. He was lean and fit, and had not seen another white man for months. He regaled the newcomers with stories into the small hours, and gave them valuable information about the area in which they hoped to travel. Raoul was intrigued by this nomad, and perhaps a little jealous of the way he had cut himself off from his conventional, public-school background to carve out a life in Africa. In the end he drifted away into the darkness, followed by cries of good wishes, and disappeared from Raoul's life for ever, 'gone with the wind, unsung and unreported'.

Two weeks and a thousand miles south of Khartoum, they left the Nile at a village called Shambe and spent one night in a ramshackle rest-house pullulating with mosquitoes and fruit bats. Finding he could not sleep, Raoul walked out onto the verandah, which was about 15 yards from the water's edge. There was no moon and the night was very dark. As he gingerly went down two steps and trod on what he thought was a substantial tree-trunk, the thing erupted and flung him into the air. The crocodile had presumably come up onto the sand to lay its eggs, and gave him a severe fright. Next day the party set out for the interior, reinforced by fifty-five stocky men of the Niam Niam tribe from the Congo, described by Johnny as 'jolly cannibals'. 'As soon as they realised we were going to look after them, and could shoot a bit, they became great friends and helpers,' Raoul recorded, 'always singing and doing music-hall turns.'

The hunters' first targets were the antelopes known as lechwe or Mrs Gray's kob, which were living in and around marshes alive with mosquitoes. When, after a long stalk in punishing heat, Raoul at last got the chance of a shot, he was standing up to his waist in bog, 'in high grass that cut like a razor', and so precariously poised that he missed with eight consecutive bullets. After running and wading for another hour under the blazing sun, he at last managed to shoot a large buck; but when he staggered back into camp at

Raoul's sketch of a Hadendowa sheikh caught something of the tribesmen's pride and independence. At a ceremonial banquet the natives offered the artist and his father, as a special delicacy, goats' eyes impaled on slivers of horn.

into the slow-moving water about 40 yards from the bank, and Mahommed immediately began stripping off, 'preparatory to emulating a field-trial labrador.'

'No, no!' cried Raoul. Crocodiles.'

11 a.m., his father described him as 'red from the bites of mosquitoes, bloody from grass cuts, and quite exhausted'.

Leaving the forest, the party struck out north-westwards across open plains which still resembled a Garden of Eden. Animals roamed everywhere and the local tribes, the deep-copper-coloured Dinka and Nuers, were as friendly as could be. The Dinka men generally went about naked, but Johnny noted 'a curious and horrible custom' which they had recently adopted: that of wearing clothes in the presence of Europeans.

Raoul was particularly delighted with their athletic prowess. Since his grandfather had been renowned for his high-jumping, he was fascinated when the Nuers staged 'an Olympic sports meeting' for the benefit of the visitors. A man 6ft tall stood with one arm raised to its full extent above his head, holding a spear out horizontally. Over this bar, which must have been more than 7ft from the ground, sprang two competitors. There was no nonsense about fancy rolls or twists: they simply took three strides, cleared the bar and landed on their feet. The Dinka also demonstrated astonishing stamina across country. When Raoul wrote a letter to his mother, a young Dinka pushed it into his cleft stick and set off for the Nile. Three days later he was back, having covered 200 miles – and he must have gone all the way, because the letter reached its destination. The Dinka could also follow spoor across brick-hard ground at great speed, without hesitation.

The only time Raoul found himself in trouble with the natives was when he spotted a crocodile sunning itself in the far bank of a river. Seeing ten or more young children splashing about in the water below it, he was horrified, and promptly shot the beast with his .256 Mannlicher. As he put it later, 'the crocodile never moved, but the village did.' Dozens of men raced out at him, yelling and brandishing spears, led by their headman in a leopardskin. Having

quickly snapped another round into the breech, he levelled his rifle at them, but luckily they stopped short, and a few exchanges through interpreters established that in their view he had shot the Chief's grandfather, whose spirit had taken up residence in the crocodile ten years earlier. When Raoul asked about the children bathing, the answer was an offhand, 'Oh, he had a couple of them last week.' With the headman placated by the gift of a few cartridges, the hunters went on their way unmolested.

A thousand miles south of Khartoum, Raoul and his father hunted their way westwards across the plains, and frequently found themselves among elephants. The great beasts, which fascinated Raoul, were happily not one of his target species.

They often slept in the open, and it was the responsibility of the 'cannibals' to keep a big fire going. Within the perimeter of its blaze there was no danger from the lions, hyenas and jackals, which patrolled in the darkness beyond, with their eyes shining in the firelight. Occasionally a porter threw a burning branch at them and they would vanish for a few minutes, only to return. But when one of the men strayed outside the security zone, he was never seen again. His companions seemed unperturbed by his disappearance, and Raoul again had to think hard about attitudes to life and death.

29

Studies of kob antelope. During the safari Raoul made several hundred drawings, but almost the only ones now preserved are those which appeared in his father's book about the trip, *Far Away up the Nile*, published in 1924.

On most mornings they broke camp at 2 o'clock, because after dawn the temperature rose alarmingly to nearly 120°F and the main anxiety of the day was always about finding water. Local guides, recruited from villages, often proved unreliable; they would stride out confidently for two or three hours, only to land the party at a mud-hole abandoned since the last rainy season and surrounded by skeletons, some of them human.

As the weeks went by, Raoul found that his body became accustomed to the heat and perpetual thirst, and he learned to live with the discomfort. Years later he recalled that he survived mainly on 'biltong, biscuits and tea', and that he never felt fitter.

Walking an average of 25 miles a day for 60 days, he reckoned that he covered at least 1,500 miles on foot. For weeks he was far out of reach of civilisation; he had no means of communication with the outside world, no method of summoning help in the event of a disaster. Yet he was perfectly content, absorbed in the magic of his surroundings. He saw elephants, lions, rhinos and hippos almost every day, and he drew hundreds of sketches of them; most of the drawings have now disappeared, but those that survive are fired by wonderful strength and life.

Elephants fascinated him particularly. If they were disturbed or given a fright, they would crash off through the bush and trees in a thunderous stampede. On the other hand, if they decided there was no hurry, the enormous, clumsy-looking creatures could filter away without a sound. Rhinos usually presented equally little problem. Raoul found that they were inquisitive but short-sighted; if they spotted humans, they would advance at a slow trot and stop about 20 yards off. If there was a suitable tree behind which he could dodge, Raoul sometimes waved a handkerchief at them to provoke a charge. When one started, the boys would yell with excitement and race across the bows of the speeding, two-ton juggernauts, like Western children playing chicken in front of cars or trains. Occasionally one was knocked over, but none of them was seriously hurt, even though the rhinos were quite unable to brake quickly, and often took at least 100 yards to pull up.

The most dangerous animal of all, Raoul decided, was the rogue male buffalo. But he also developed a burning hatred of crocodiles, because they preyed on the helpless women and children who had to come down to the rivers every morning for water. One day, at the urgent behest of a village headman and his councillors, he shot three monsters; they towed one ashore before it sank, and found it was over 20ft long. When they slit it open, they discovered that its belly was full of bangles, bracelets and beads.

His most traumatic experience was with bees. An old bull buffalo had gone on the rampage; ostracised from the herd, he had taken to attacking the inhabitants of a nearby village, and Raoul promised to try to kill him. With two of his followers he tracked the animal into the forest and shot him dead, thereby both eliminating the threat and providing meat for the next week at least.

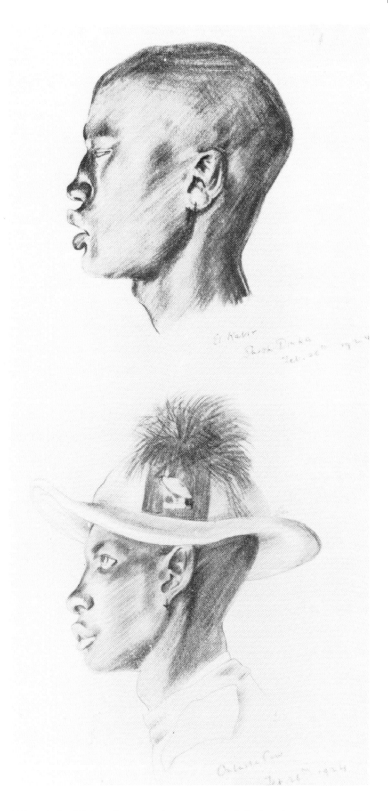

Although the Dinka tribesmen who accompanied the hunting party normally went about naked, Raoul's father noticed that some of them had recently adopted the 'curious and horrible custom' of wearing clothes in the presence of Europeans.

31

When the buffalo went down, the local people, who had been hanging about behind bushes, gave him an ovation 'as if Malmesbury had scored a goal against Arsenal'.

Hardly had he begun skinning the animal so that he could cut up the meat for distribution among the rollicking fans, however, when suddenly a loud hum increased to a roar as bees poured down onto the carcass by the thousand, seeking the blood. Raoul had heard many stories of attacks by killer bees: humans stung to death, blinded, driven into rivers and drowned. Looking round, he saw that his supporters had vanished. What was he to do?

For most of his sentient life, at home and at school, the importance of keeping calm had been drilled into him. Now his long training bore fruit. Moving as little and as gently as possible, he continued with his task. In fact he had little alternative, as hundreds of bees were already crawling over his bare arms and legs. By the time he had finished – without a single sting – most of the swarm had dropped off the carcass, sated with blood, or flown away, and Raoul returned to camp with a singing, dancing escort. When Johnny heard what had happened, he said, 'Good. You're obviously a survivor.' But Raoul had never been so frightened for so long.

All went reasonably well until 6 February, when the party reached the village of Rumbek; but there in the rest-house father and son were stricken with diarrhoea and sickness. A local Syrian doctor gave them each an immense dose of castor oil, a remedy which soon cured Raoul, but left Johnny racked by dysentery. Raoul suggested that they should return to the Nile, more than 100 miles to the east, but Johnny was determined that his son should secure that 'blue ribbon' of big game, a giant eland, and so they continued westwards towards the Gelle River, the father on a donkey, the son on his feet.

In the course of the next two weeks, Raoul achieved his ambi-

Poshto! Dinkas celebrate the slaughter of a buffalo and the arrival of meat. The Millais, father and son, were thrilled by the athletic prowess of these natives, who could jump more than their own height from a standing start.

tion and had several more thrilling encounters with buffalo, but the time was one of acute anxiety. While he stalked and hunted on his own, his father lay sweating and shaking in tents or huts, so ill that at one point he remembered nothing for seventy-two hours on end. For day after day Raoul was convinced that he was going to die, yet Johnny would not hear of returning to the Nile until an eland was in the bag.

Raoul never forgot his intense excitement when a tall man clad in a leopardskin and carrying a spear appeared in the firelight one night. A professional tracker, the stranger said he could find the elusive eland, so he and Raoul set off before dawn. After about 10 miles the guide stopped and pointed at the hard ground, but Raoul could see nothing. Later the man halted again and broke a leaf from a bush. This time Raoul *could* see something: saliva. Soon the guide stopped for the third time and pointed excitedly with his spear.

A hundred yards ahead, something moved in the bush: the swishing tail of a cow eland. Suddenly the whole thicket erupted and about fifty animals streamed out at a fast trot. Remembering stories about how eland, once started, may run for 50 miles, Raoul set off after them. Luckily for him, they stopped after only a mile or so, and a very large bull with a huge head turned to look at his pursuers. Raoul was heaving with exhaustion, but he thought, 'It's now or never', and a lucky shot took the antelope in the neck, dropping him where he stood. Elated, Raoul aimed at another big bull moving to his left, and dropped that too. The porters were no less excited, for eland meat was reckoned the best in Africa, and there was wild singing and dancing on the way back to camp.

By the time the party returned towards Rumbek on 22 February, Johnny was too weak even to ride, so four stout Niam Niams carried him in a litter. Ever since he was taken ill, he had been sending out messengers in search of fresh milk – the one remedy, he felt certain, which would put paid to the dysentery. When they reached the village, Raoul at last found some of the longed-for elixir. Johnny drank it, and in the morning reported that his dysentery had gone.

As he lay in bed for a couple of days, recovering his strength, he reported that the heat was 'like a blast furnace', but his spirits rose enough for him to compose a facetious advertisement for Rumbek, such as might adorn railway station platforms in England. Signing himself 'Professor Fathead, FRS', he urged tourists:

Come to glorious Rumbek! The Cheltenham of Central Africa! An eighteen-hole golf course is under construction. Caddies used to crocodiles assist at the burn. The hippopotami make excellent bunkers . . .

Hardly had he written that when he went down with a high fever, which he supposed was malaria, and he had to make his way

The graceful lechwe, also known as Mrs Gray's Kob, were living in marshes alive with mosquitoes. The heads obtained by Raoul went back to swell his father's world-famous collection of big-game trophies, later much coveted by Ernest Hemingway.

back to the Nile by road, being offered lifts by various well-wishers. Raoul continued mainly on foot, shooting as he went, and the two were reunited in Shambe, where they embarked on a steamer and headed downriver for Khartoum. For Johnny the eight-day trip was a nightmare, since his fever grew ever worse, and he reached the capital 'in a state of collapse'.

The news there was alarming: the Sirdar, Sir Lee Stack, had been murdered by a terrorist during a visit to Cairo. Closer at hand there had been a lesser tragedy. When Raoul asked Brock about Sayed, the big lion in the zoo, there was an ominous silence. Then Brock let on that the head keeper had taken a fat Egyptian friend into the enclosure while the lion was lying asleep. The Egyptian, having

killed him at the age of sixty-five.

His book about the trip, *Far Away up the Nile*, was published towards the end of 1924. He himself did some of the pictures for it, but the bulk of the illustrations were taken from drawings made by Raoul. Very fine they are, too: full of movement and delicacy, but also conveying the bulk and strength of elephants, buffaloes and antelopes.

That same year, 1924, Johnny decided that he needed one more head for his museum – that of the giant sable antelope, which lived in a remote corner of Angola, in south-west Africa. He himself was not well enough to face another expedition, so he sent Raoul on

When Raoul shot a rogue male buffalo which had been harassing the inhabitants of a village, the locals were beside themselves with excitement, and gave him an ovation 'as if Malmesbury had scored a goal against Arsenal.'

heard how tame the animal was, stalked up to him and opened his umbrella with a snap, right in his face – and that was that. The keeper managed to escape, but the remains of the stout *effendi* were swept up with dustpan and brush.

In the City Hospital an injection of quinine brought Johnny's temperature down from 104° to normal and enabled him to face the two-week voyage home; but although he thought he was cured, he had in fact contracted blackwater fever, probably from drinking the milk, and in the end, seven years later, the disease

his own, with £250 to cover all expenses. Angola was then a colony administered by the Portuguese, who were making it difficult for foreigners to enter the country, but Johnny wrote to the Portuguese Ambassador in London and got Raoul a special *laisser-passer*. Moreover, he had a key contact in the form of an engineer called Varian, who had been building the railway that ran from the Angolan coast up to the great copper mines of Rhodesia. Varian had left, by then, but he put his bungalow on the coast at Raoul's disposal.

Raoul, of course, 'couldn't wait to start'. He took passage on a German ship, the *Usaramo*, sailing from Southampton to Cape Town, and calling at Lisbon, the Ivory Coast, and Luanda (the capital) and Lobito in Angola. The other passengers consisted mostly of Portuguese and Germans, Raoul being the only Englishman on board.

At Luanda he was taken ashore by a lady 'of outsize proportions', said to have been exiled from Portugal for knifing her lover. This large person introduced Raoul to the governor of the local prison, a horrific institution whose cells had been carved out of a cliff over-looking the bay. The inmates on the lowest floor were chained to the walls, so that at high tide the sea came up to their necks. The governor assured Raoul that no man had ever escaped, and no man had lived for five years. Altogether it was a depressing introduction to what turned out to be one huge penal colony.

At Lobito Raoul was met by an agent of Varian's, who told him he must slip the Customs a substantial bribe, along with half his tobacco and cigars, otherwise there would be no hope of seeing his rifle and ammu-nition again. This naked corruption gave Raoul a shock, as did the barriers of wire netting around the bungalow in which he stayed. When he asked what they were for, the answer was to keep out the rats, which carried bubonic plague.

The railway line up-country was still being built – by a British firm –

Head of the giant eland, the Blue Riband of big game and most elusive of quarries, which Raoul pursued for days in the company of a native tracker wearing a leopardskin, after his father had been laid low by blackwater fever.

and reached only 400 miles to a temporary railhead. Raoul boarded the one first-class carriage and found himself the sole occupant of this 'Claridges on wheels.' Woken at dawn next morning by screams and shouts, he found the train at a standstill, and descended to discover a lion asleep on the points in front of the engine. When he dislodged it with a well-aimed piece of wood, the train exploded into cheers, and he found himself a reluctant hero 'for the second time since prep-school days' (the other was when he stopped the runaway horses).

At the railhead he met the resident chief engineer, an Englishman, who gave him valuable advice, and in particular warned him on no account to buy or accept diamonds during his trek, since news of any transac-tion would travel ahead of him by bush telegraph, and he would inevitably be arrested by the police. On Raoul's behalf the engineer had collected a gang of porters from the Chimbundu tribe, led by a foreman called Vindula, who spoke a few words of French. In spite of his amazing get-up – a black velvet smoking jacket, a pair of army-issue boots hung round his neck by the laces and a hat made from a yellow cardboard box with DUNLOP TUBE emblazoned across the front – Vindula proved an effective and utterly loyal lieutenant.

A few days later, after the party had advanced 100 miles into the unknown northern terri-tories, Raoul, sure enough, was offered two immense blue diamonds the size of thrushes' eggs by the chief of a village. These, said the chief, would be his if he would stay as the honoured guest of the villagers and defend them against the police, whose habit it was to come and seize young men for forced labour.

Remembering the engineer's warning, Raoul declined with thanks, but accepted an alternative proposal: that he should present the chief with six of his .275 Mauser rifle cartridges. Since the chief owned only a muzzle-loader, it was not clear what use he would make of the sophisticated ammunition, but the deal was concluded, everyone was happy, and the chief provided a guide for the main phase of Raoul's sable hunt.

This took some time, but Raoul was able to put to good use the experience of tracking which he had gained in the Sudan, and in the course of three weeks he obtained two very fine heads. With them in the bag, he set out on the long trek back to the railhead. One afternoon, when he was within 10 miles of journey's end, he saw a motley crew of armed police, in ragged uniforms and led by a sergeant, coming towards them.

When Vindula said something to the leader of the posse, the sergeant hit him across the face with the butt of his rifle and knocked him flat. After a long, hot day, this was too much. Raoul lost his temper, picked the sergeant up and threw him into the river, followed by his rifle. He then levelled the .275 at the remaining rabble, who hesitated for a moment, looking shocked, but then bolted.

The British engineer later told him that the men almost certainly had no ammunition, as they could not be trusted not to fire on their own officers. Summoned to an interview by the district commissioner, Raoul avoided paying a fine by the simple expedient of walking out while the man was on the telephone.

A more disturbing incident took place in the compound at the railhead, where a captive male baboon which normally lived tethered to a pole had broken its chain and taken refuge on the ridge of a roof. Raoul has never liked apes, feeling that they are 'sinister and sometimes menacing characters, and very unpredictable . . . Shades of my old nanny, perhaps'. Nevertheless he coaxed the baboon down, but suddenly the animal leapt onto him with its arms round his neck and its face glued to his left cheek, chattering and shivering with fright. For about ten minutes the two remained locked in this potentially dangerous embrace, watched from a safe distance by the crowd until, by talking quietly, Raoul at last persuaded the baboon to relax its grip and return to its former station at the foot of the pole.

He paid off his porters at the railhead, but Vindula accompanied him back to the coast at Lobito, where he found he had to wait ten days for the next Union-Castle liner. The prospect of the delay did not worry him, as he looked forward to working on drawings and writing up his diary. But he made the grave mistake of buying an orange from a fruit stall at the station, and within twenty-four hours he was down with acute diarrhoea and fever.

The faithful Vindula looked after him as best he could, bringing goat's milk and sitting by his bed. But Raoul had to endure nine days of dreadful discomfort, his misery exacerbated by pop-eyed rats which scurried about the floor of the bungalow and sometimes invaded his bed. When at last he was carried aboard the ship, his weight had gone down from its normal 13 stone 7lb to little over 9 stone. He gave Vindula everything he had – 'quite inade-

quate payment for his loyalty' – and the two had an emotional farewell.

Raoul's mother, meeting him at Southampton, was horrified by his appearance and rushed him to hospital, where doctors diagnosed amoebic dysentery and typhoid. The source, they said, must have been the orange he ate in Lobito – and he has never been able to face one since.

Raoul with the horns of a giant sable antelope, the principal target during his trip to Angola in 1924-25. By the time he reached home, acute dysentery and fever had reduced his weight from its normal 13 stone 7lb to little over 9 stone.

Head of a Hadendowa tribesman, sketched during Raoul's first trip to Africa in 1924. It was members of this tribe, known as 'fuzzy-wuzzies' from their crinkly hair, who broke the enemy square at the battle of Omdurman in 1898.

CHAPTER FIVE

HORSES AND HUNTING

At a hunt ball in 1923, before he left on his first trip to Africa, Raoul had met a girl of striking dark looks called Clare Macdonell, who was one year older than him. He was greatly taken with her and asked if she would marry him. When she agreed, he was forced to divulge that he was about to leave the country for several months. Would she wait for him to return? She would.

Clare's mother was Irish, a Ryan from County Tipperary, but on her father's side she was descended from a family who had emigrated to Canada from the West Coast of Scotland in 1745. Her father, the engineer A.J. Macdonell, had built the Canadian Pacific Railway through the Rockies, and also many canals in Florida. When railways took over as the main method of freight transport in the south, the canals became obsolete and the Florida company seemed worthless. After Macdonell's death in 1901, his widow found a trunk full of canal share certificates in the attic and looked on them as a bad joke – until she discovered that the family owned a 100-yard strip of land on either side of each waterway, and since a property boom had set in, they were millionaires.

When she came to Europe in 1904, she did so in style, sailing on the *Empress of Canada*, and bringing not only her eight children, along with a squad of nannies and governesses, but also an ice-yacht and her personal train. In due course she bought Frimley Park, a large house in Surrey, and the girls were sent to Roehampton.

Raoul never met Mrs Macdonell, who died in 1924; but Clare was not one to make empty promises. Having said she would wait for Raoul, she did. The couple were married in Brompton Oratory, in London, in 1925, and a Macdonell family trust helped them buy a fine seventeenth-century Cotswold farmhouse called Farleaze, nicely tucked away down its own lane near Malmesbury,

in Wiltshire (Raoul's father paid half the purchase price). There they settled, and Raoul launched into an existence which most country people could only dream about.

Never going to an office, never commuting to a city, he worked at home and earned his living by painting horses. At first, of course, bucolic hunting types found it distinctly unnerving to have an artist in their midst. One evening, as Raoul was hacking homewards after a day with the Duke of Beaufort's hounds, Lieutenant-Colonel Guy Hanmer rode up beside him and said, 'You the painter fellow?' Raoul agreed, and for a few minutes the two rode on in silence. Then Hanmer said, 'You must agree, old boy: I mean, it's *damned odd* for a fellow to paint.'

Those words exactly caught the apprehension of Raoul's neighbours, who could not quite place the new arrival. To them an artist was a creature with a beard, a beret, a smock and a floppy tie, who lived in a city and understood nothing about rural pursuits. When they found that *this* artist wore normal country clothes, lived in a farmhouse and himself hunted several days a week, they could not reconcile the reality with their preconceptions. Nevertheless, when they discovered how he could ride, and saw what sort of pictures he painted, they soon came to accept him.

As his fame spread, so did his invitations: for the next twelve years he hunted with many of the most famous packs in England – the Beaufort, the Berkeley, the VWH Cricklade, the Quorn, the Heythrop, the Meynell, the Pytchley, the Woodland Pytchley, the Croome, the North Yorks and Ainsty, the Middleton, the Sinnington, the Crawley and Horsham, the Southdown, the Avon Vale, the Blackmore Vale, the Bathurst, the Tidworth. Wherever he went, he was welcomed as much for his enthusiasm, his genial presence and his unfailing courtesy as for his artistic achievement.

Such was his skill, and so easily did he fit into the hunting environment, that many of his clients asked him to come and stay, either bringing his own horses with him or hunting theirs. And never did a commission have happier consequences than one to paint the wife of an elderly member of the Quorn. Since she rode side-saddle – as did most women before the war – and was very

OPPOSITE:
Raoul's chestnut gelding Garland, one of the best hunters he ever owned, being led by Pat Shortall, the Irish groom who worked at Farleaze between the wars, with Polly the lurcher in close attendance.

Mary, Duchess of Beaufort, hunting side-saddle on Domino, painted in 1928. After some initial tiffs, Raoul came to like her husband, the tenth Duke, known in his country as 'Master', and the two men remained friends for life.

elegant, with a long, straight back, she made an ideal subject; better still was the fact that the family collected blood horses, and had eighteen in the yard. The husband rode one and the wife two, so there were fifteen spare, all schooled by a splendid head lad, a rough-rider who was a genius at his job. For the whole of that season Raoul hunted two days a week, with two horses out each day, and so gained a lifelong love of the Quorn country, which then was almost entirely grass.

In retrospect, he saw the Quorn as the country of his dreams. If the scent was poor, the huntsman would pick up the hounds and gallop for miles, followed by an enthusiastic field who had no idea

OPPOSITE:
Hunters and racehorses became Raoul's main subjects between the world wars, but he went through a phase of painting stylish carriages, which had impressed him tremendously as a boy growing up at Compton's Brow, his parents' home near Horsham.

that they were chasing thin air. One day the Master, Chatty Hilton Green, riding beside Raoul, looked over a hedge and cried, 'Good God! We can't have that! I'll be back in a minute.' Away he galloped to a nearby farmhouse, and when he returned he said in tones of outrage, 'That field's been ploughed! I told the farmer we can't have that sort of thing here. It's got to go back to grass next year.'

Farleaze proved an ideal base, being close to that fox-hunting Mecca, Badminton, home of the Dukes of Beaufort. The tenth duke, commonly known as Master, was a commanding figure, whom many people found autocratic and difficult. Raoul considered him 'really a very nice man, but perhaps rather far down the list for Brain of Britain,' and made proper contact with him by the classic method of standing up for himself when the Duke tried to bully him.

On Saturdays the Beaufort field could be over 400 strong, and everyone was expected to go through gates rather than jump fences. In Raoul's view the gates were far more dangerous than walls or hedges, as the mob which was jammed up and struggling to get through always included several horses which kicked, and casualties were frequent. Raoul was one of a group of five or six young thrusters known as 'the Bolsheviks,' who liked having a go across country; and one day, after somebody had committed the offence of jumping into a field of winter corn, Master rode up to Raoul and cursed him in front of the whole field. When Raoul explained that he was not the culprit, the Duke called him a liar and sent him home. Raoul sat down and wrote an exceedingly rude letter, which, 'to his eternal credit', Master answered with four pages of apology.

Thereafter the two became friends. In 1928 Raoul painted the duke's wife Mary galloping side-saddle in the famous Beaufort colours of blue coat with buff facings. If the picture lacks the artist's usual grace – the rider has a hard, unfeminine look about her, and the horse, Domino, has a hideous face, mostly white – it may have helped to cement relations. In any case, Raoul did an etching of the duke hunting hounds, and later, when the two met at Pirbright during the Second World War, they played cricket together and reminisced happily about old times.

On days when Captain Maurice Kingscote, Field Master of the Beaufort, was in control, the atmosphere was less volatile, for he never shouted at delinquents, keeping everyone in check by means of charm and diplomacy. When he went on to become Master of the Meynell and South Atherstone, he often asked Raoul to stay, and always mounted him on a good horse. Raoul described him as 'a man without much money but a heart of gold,' who sold more

'Elegant Figures in a Park'. Another echo of Raoul's childhood, when his mother constantly took him and his sister to parties and receptions, often driving in horse-drawn carriages.

horses than the artist sold pictures, and could persuade any city tycoon to buy a suspect donkey to win the Grand National.

Only once did Raoul find somebody who had outmanoeuvred the captain. Hacking home one day, he found himself next to a man named Rabbits, mounted on a nice roan cob.

'That's a good sort of horse,' Raoul observed.

'I know,' said Rabbits. 'I bought it from Captain Kingscote. But to start with I put it about that I was in the market for several expensive horses. I knew the first one he sold me would be a cracker – and I only want one, because I only hunt on Saturdays.'

When it came to buying horses for himself, Raoul set a top price of £200, which often meant that he ended up with a failed race

'The Forge'. During a day's hunting, a rider discusses some problem – almost
certainly a cast shoe – with the blacksmith. A scene remembered from Raoul's
many days in Ireland.

horse, or an animal 'that had put his owner in hospital once too often'. There were generally bargains to be had at Tattersall's sales in Newmarket, where he had friends who could warn him how great a risk he might be taking on – 'how lethal the bet might be.' Only once did he buy a horse which had actually killed its previous owner – a feat he did not hear about until later. Their first day out hunting, the animal went straight through a post-and-rail fence at speed, shooting Raoul into the next field. The horse then picked itself up, turned round and came charging back at its rider with teeth bared.

Raoul at the gate of Farleaze, the sixteenth-century farmhouse near Malmesbury where he and his first wife Clare lived between the wars. From here, an ideal base, he hunted with the Duke of Beaufort's and many other packs.

Another, bought for £35, had been hunted by the Huntsman of the Leconfield Hounds, and made a whistle 'like the 4.30 from Paddington.' Out for exercise, Raoul leant forward in the saddle to open a five-barred gate, whereupon the horse jumped the obstacle from a standstill. Next day came a letter from the previous owner saying that, in spite of the whistle, the horse was the best he'd ever had, and would jump anything. 'But for God's sake,' it ended, 'don't try to open a gate with him.' In spite of that quirk, Raoul hunted the horse for several seasons, and he never refused or fell.

A favourite source of cheap mounts was Ireland, where Raoul had friends with ears to the turf and whence, every now and then, a message would emanate. 'There's a hell of a blood horse in Tipperary. Only three. As tall as a tree, to suit your long legs, and a furious lepper, besides. Better get over here quick . . .'

His best-ever Irish buy was Hunter's Moon, a huge thorough-bred mare, 17 hands high and four years old, whom he got from a racing stable in County Tipperary for £150. On the track she had never finished better than fourth, but when Raoul brought her back to England and took her hunting, she proved an outright winner. He hunted her for five seasons all over England and Wales: she never went lame, and the only time she fell was when he jumped her over a post-and-rails onto a tarmac road. There she stood on her head, and Raoul, landing hands first, sprained both thumbs. He painted a glorious picture of her, glossy with health, standing in a courtyard beneath a Spanish lantern, with an elegant stone archway beyond.

One of Raoul's most memorable hunts with the Beaufort was from Jackaments Bottom, a long, narrow valley which runs parallel to the road from Cirencester to Tetbury. Being away up in the far north of the country, it was not a fashionable rendezvous, and only forty or fifty people turned out; but there was a roaring scent, and hounds went away like an express train, past the covert called George's Gorse and the Troublehouse Inn, a pub on the main road. Raoul was riding Garland, a magnificent chestnut who was very fast and would tackle any obstacle.

For the first two or three miles they met mostly walls, which Garland flew; then they jumped down into an unmarked stone quarry, down the side of which he slid on his backside. Emerging unscathed, they roared on flat out for another seven or eight miles until they found themselves in the Berkeley Vale, with its big open ditches known as reens, and its brush fences. There the hounds killed their fox after a point of at least 10 miles.

Looking back, Raoul reckoned Garland was the best horse he ever had. When they went together on hunting/painting visits to the Pytchley country or to Yorkshire, people offered large sums for him. But to his owner he was like a pet dog, appearing to understand everything said to him. When Raoul chatted to him on their way home from a day's hunting, he would twitch back his ears and nod his head, and whenever they stopped at a pub, he would down a pint of beer (which his rider hated) with the greatest relish. For Raoul to paint a self-portrait was extremely rare, but he did one of himself on Garland, out with the Beaufort, in which the rider is all long leg, straight back and flying tails. A second fine painting shows Garland being led by Pat Shortall, the Irish groom who worked at Farleaze throughout the twenties and thirties, with Polly the lurcher following.

Another star, almost in the same class, was Greyman, a big, rangy horse four years old but hardly backed, which Raoul found on a

OPPOSITE:
'Four Stallions being Led'. Like many of Raoul's pictures, this does not represent any particular scene that he witnessed, but is an amalgam of different images. Racing clouds, flying manes and the attitudes of the horses give a fine impression of the wind.

mountain in County Tipperary. His owner had fallen ill and left him to a farmer, who did not know what to do with him. So, for £120, Raoul acquired a natural hunter which for five seasons carried him everywhere, never falling, never going lame.

The origins of Kingfisher, his third favourite, were entirely different. He belonged to a rich American woman who lived in Leicestershire, and who summoned Raoul to paint her in the saddle. When Raoul arrived, he found the horse had gone lame; the vet had told the owner that the problem was incurable and the horse should be put down. The stud groom said this was nonsense: the horse was only shin-sore. Having painted his picture, Raoul proposed that he should swap it for the horse. The owner protested that this would be grossly unfair, but in the end accepted the bargain. Raoul rested Kingfisher in a boggy field all summer, got him sound and hunted him everywhere.

The Millais' first son, John, was born in April 1927, and their second, Hugh, in December 1929. Like Compton's Brow, Farleaze was an ideal environment for boys with country bents. The house had a big garden, including a fine water garden fed by a small stream which ran beneath the lawn; but beyond the cultivated area lay 150 acres of wild land, unfarmed except for one field on which hay was made. The rest of the ground was rough grass dotted with scrub and thorn bushes, all full of rabbits. Sixty years later, Johnny remembered how, if he spotted one sitting in a tussock, he could sometimes drop on it and catch it with his hands.

He also recalled how, when he was eight or nine, Raoul came on him and Hugh indoors, reading books, one fine afternoon. 'My God!' he cried. 'What the hell are you doing? Get out! At your age I'd have been shooting.'

The children lived what Hugh later described as 'very much a green-baize-door existence', being looked after by nannies for most of the time and 'brought into the drawing room polished up for an hour after tea'. Yet Raoul loved romping with them when they were small; he would pull the cushions off the sofa and rag on the floor until bedlam reigned. In summer, after lunch, he would play croquet with them on the lawn. A favourite indoor game was 'Squiggles', in which one of the boys would make a squiggle on a piece of paper, and with a few deft touches Raoul would convert it into some ridiculous creature, like a stoat riding a bicycle.

Being very sociable, Raoul and Clare not only entertained a good deal, but frequently went to stay with friends, driving off (in Hugh's memory) 'in huge cars, wearing leather helmets, and with masses of luggage'. To Hugh, life at Farleaze seemed like 'one long party in the Beaufort country'.

Always the professional, Raoul worked long hours in his studio, and as his fame increased, requests for pictures built up so fast that

at one stage he had bookings five years ahead. By the mid-1930s he was charging up to £500 per painting – a large amount in those days. To minimise the time he kept people and horses standing around, he developed a photographic eye and memory, using quick sketches and notes to register basic information. Often he had three or four pictures on the go at once: after a couple of days' work on one, he would put it aside and not look at it again for a fortnight.

Winning racehorses and favourite hunters were his bread and butter, but he also had a phase of painting horse-drawn carriages, which had made a strong impression on him as a child, and which he considered 'tremendously romantic and elegant'. Another image which often appears in his pictures is a striped beach-hut. One friend noticed so many instances of this that he asked Raoul if it hinted at some long-gone romantic assignation: the answer was that the artist had seen huts of that kind on the beach at Bognor when he was six or seven, and that their pleasing appearance had stuck in his mind ever since.

Nor was it only in England that Raoul hunted. He had many wild adventures in Wales, acting as whipper-in to his friend George Coventry, Master of the Carmarthenshire, and charging about that rough country on 'an endless supply of sure-footed horses', mostly by a thoroughbred stallion out of Pembrokeshire pack mares, of the sort that used to carry the wool from Wales. One November day, when a hound went over a cliff, George thought it might have landed on a ledge; so he had himself lowered on a rope, and came up not only with the hound undamaged, but with two wooden eggs which he had found in a peregrine's eyrie, with the falcon still sitting on them. Even in those days, egg-thieves were active.

Raoul also frequently crossed the water to Ireland, sometimes to buy a sure-fire Grand National winner, but more often to hunt, and he loved the days spent scrambling over rough banks and ditches in the company of a handful of farmers; but he resolutely maintained that the Irish had no sense of humour. Instead, he claimed, their outlook was totally logical, and in defence of this theory he could quote any number of examples. One came up when he was fishing on the Blackwater and asked Batt Flynn, the ghillie, about a fine Georgian house standing far away on a hill.

'Would you like to live there?' Batt asked.

'There's such a long drive,' Raoul answered. 'I couldn't afford to repair it.'

'Ah, sure,' the ghillie replied. 'But if it was any shorter, it wouldn't reach the front door.'

When Raoul collapsed with laughter, Batt looked dismayed and asked anxiously, 'Have I said something wrong, Sorr?'

Another time, shooting snipe, he became irritated because Batt's black spaniel Chance was working too far ahead. Having just shot a snipe, he said, 'For God's sake get that dog back here.' To which Batt replied, 'What's the use? Sure an' if he had been here, dat bird would have been down his troat before it hit the deck.'

Again, on his way to paint a master of foxhounds in Kildare, Raoul complained about the car he was hiring in Dublin, an aged Ford Consul, which had only two forward gears which worked. 'What more do you want?' cried the manager of the firm. 'In Dublin, for God's sake stay in first, or you'll mow down a pile of drunks. But when you get into the country, change into top, and by St Peter, you'll be flying!' When Raoul brought the car back at the end of his stay, the man congratulated him on his safe return, removed a rusty pin which had been threaded through the stalk of the accelerator pedal to keep the maximum speed down to 40 mph, and said, 'Now I'll just have a look under the bonnet. They sometimes bring them back without engines.'

In England, Raoul's reputation continued to grow; but patrons were not always as tactful as they might be. 'Nice frame,' said one man. 'Can I have the address of your framers?' Another asked why he did not try sculpture, and often, when a picture was finished, his subjects asked if he would put their alsatian or pack of chihuahuas into the foreground.

One woman, described by Raoul as 'a rather vulgar millionaire, dripping in diamonds and owning several racehorses, but having no idea of the difference between a Derby prospect and a seaside donkey', commissioned a painting of one of her winners. When Raoul took it round to hand it over, she started to lay down the precise dimensions that sporting works should take, even before she had set eyes on it. 'Now,' she began, 'I know about these pictures: the bottom of the horse's hooves must be exactly two and a half inches from the bottom of the canvas, and the top of the jockey's head eight inches from the top.'

'In that case,' Raoul replied, 'I'm afraid you'll be disappointed by my measurements. But maybe you'll like the picture anyway.'

The woman's husband winked at Raoul and took the painting off into his study. Later he wrote a charming letter of apology and appreciation.

Perhaps his most tiresome patron was Viscount Mountgarret, who frequently invited him to hunt in Yorkshire, and once asked him to paint the North York and Ainsty hounds, which he hunted for some years. After days of work, during which Raoul painted individual portraits of the hounds, his host said to him after dinner, 'I say, let's change the order a bit. Let's put Ranter and Ranger in the lead, and show Royster in the middle.' Raoul demurred, pointing out that they had spent hours in the kennels deciding on the order, and he proposed to stick to it. Later he realised that Mountgarret's real purpose in chopping and changing was to keep him on the premises; being a lonely man with few friends, he

An excursion into the grotesque: Raoul's vision of Jorrocks, the immortal, irrepressible hunting grocer created by R.S.Surtees. One of his favourite maxims, echoed by countless owners, was 'Damn all presents what eats!'

longed to have somebody to whom he could talk.

Occasionally a patron was so obtuse that Raoul cast charm aside and let the Millais steel at the centre of his character flash out. A high-powered tycoon asked for a picture of his recent winner at Epsom, with the stands in the background. Raoul said that he could not paint stands or racecourses, and the man replied, 'Oh, well. Go ahead, then.' Later, when Raoul produced the painting at the tycoon's London penthouse, he said, 'Since you haven't put the stands in, I propose to knock off half the fee.'

'Right,' replied Raoul. 'In that case I'll knock off half the canvas – with which he put his foot through it. The client was horrified and protested, 'I liked the *horse*,' but by that time Raoul was walking out. The old housekeeper, who had been eavesdropping at the door, whispered, 'Wonderful! He's the nastiest man I've ever worked for.'

'Hunters at Grass'. Dearly loving his own horses, Raoul would paint them affectionately at all seasons of the year, not least during their summer lay-off.

Visits to studs or racing stables sometimes proved nerve-racking, because trainers and managers were jumpy about letting their valuable charges stand around in the open for long periods, especially during cold weather. This meant that Raoul had to fix all the necessary information in his head or jot it down in his sketchbook during one session, or at the most two. (He always found photographs dangerous, and used them only for identifying the exact shape of white or coloured markings.) In general he was depressed by the Alcatraz-like conditions in which racehorses live, confined to their boxes for twenty-three hours a day with nothing to look at but the weaving heads of other horses across the yard. On the other hand, he warmed to the trainers and stable hands, believing that contact with horses has a strongly beneficial effect on human beings.

Many trainers, when told by an owner that an artist was coming to paint one of the horses, received him with unconcealed suspicion. Like the denizens of the Beaufort country, they were visibly taken aback when they saw that their visitor looked a normal countryman.

Frank Furlong, son of the owner, up, and then with the 1936 winning jockey, Fulke Walwyn, in the saddle. (Both young men were in the 9th Lancers, in company with Raoul's brother-in-law Ronald Macdonell.)

An equally celebrated subject was Blue Peter, winner of the

One enjoyable racing engagement was to paint Reynoldstown, who won the Grand National two years running, in 1935 and 1936. In the eyes of the artist, this great horse had 'all the assets required in the perfect conformation of a steeplechaser,' and in keeping with his achievement, Raoul painted him twice, first with

ABOVE: The Duchess of Roxburghe, riding without a hat through one of Raoul's Arcadian landscapes. Elizabeth, wife of the ninth Duke ('Bobo'), was a good friend of the Millais family.

OPPOSITE: Greyskin, seen here with Mira the springer spaniel, survived unscathed when he put his foot in a hole out hunting and went head over heels. But the fall broke Raoul's neck, and effectively ended his hunting career.

1939 Derby, painted for his owner, Lord Rosebery. His lordship was delighted with the picture and, as Raoul was going to be away, asked if he could call to fetch it next day from the Millais' flat in London. Raoul's wife, who made the rendezvous, thought he said he would come at noon. In fact he said 'nine', and arrived when she was still in bed, catching up on some sleep after a late party.

A rare self-portrait of the artist in action: with his long legs, straight back, top hat and easy seat, Raoul cuts a stylish figure on his favourite hunter Garland.

When she went to answer the bell and saw a large man standing there, she thought it was probably a thief, so she slammed the door in his face. All was resolved when Rosebery shouted his identity through the letter-box, and she invited him in for coffee, eggs and bacon.

Hunting was by no means the only sport at which Raoul excelled. His accuracy and style as a game shot became legendary; he would shoot driven pheasants quickly and without apparent effort, keeping his left arm straight and rarely missing. For some reason, however, he found that shooting and painting did not mix, and he never painted pictures of the shooting field. Nor did fishing attract him as a subject; an excellent fly-fisherman himself, on clear chalk streams as well as on Highland and Norwegian rivers, he left the depiction of piscatorial activity to others.

He never claimed that he could teach anyone to paint or draw. A fervent admirer of Stubbs, he maintained that he himself learned by trial and error, 'mostly the latter'. In a rare piece of advice to young artists in his field he once wrote, 'If you become fairly proficient, you can make a commercial success', but he also warned against the danger of 'getting stuck in a financial rut, which stops any talent stone dead. There is always this dilemma facing one, between art and finance, and one continually has to make decisions.' As to technique, he advised, 'Don't get stuck with the profile facing left to right. Experiment with action. You can use dramatic skies, figures, trees and different landscapes to add interest and avoid stereotypes.'

Those were his own methods, and never were they better deployed than in his painting of Greyskin, a point-to-pointer which he bought in 1933. The purchase was a saga in itself. Raoul had a friend called Dick Howell, who lived in a remote cottage in the Welsh mountains 'with a pack of rough hounds and a pair of Purdey shotguns, but singularly lacking in the other essentials of life, the foremost being money.' Hearing one day that Dick was in trouble, Raoul drove deep into Wales and arrived in the evening to find him huddled over a bare table with their mutual friend George Coventry.

'Come in, come in!' cried Dick. 'They're making me bankrupt in the morning. The bailiffs are coming in to hold an auction of everything I've got.'

'Gone Away'. Hounds accelerate out of covert and hit off the line as a fox breaks to the left: a typical hunting scene, recreated not from sketches, but from images stored in Raoul's amazingly retentive mind.

Hunter's Moon, 17 hands high and one of Raoul's best mares, came from a racing stable in Co. Tipperary, where he bought her for £150. She had never won a race in Ireland, but carried him tirelessly through five hunting seasons.

Mares and foals: a typically peaceful summer scene, all warm sunlight and greenery.

Having decided that this was intolerable, the other two spent the next couple of hours digging a hole in the hillside, in which they secreted the Purdeys and some pieces of silver – the only objects of value. Next morning the bailiffs duly arrived, but so also did many farmer friends who were prepared to buy things up and give them back to Dick as soon as the auction was over.

In the paddock was what Raoul described as 'a stuffy sort of a grey horse with a short back and an unusually deep body'. He was called Greyskin, and had allegedly won twenty out of twenty-two point-to-point races in Wales, often trying to go round the course again. Raoul bought him for £35, even though Dick warned him that the horse had a mouth like a steel trap: 'Once he's made up his mind to go, a brick wall won't stop him.'

Back in Beaufort country, the truth of the remark was soon apparent. On his first day out Raoul quickly realised that he was 'an unwilling passenger, with no control whatever.' He managed

to steer the horse away from hounds, but they covered six fields and cleared half a dozen obstacles before he could pull up. Thereafter he rode Greyskin in a special bit, a Balding gag, and just about managed to assert his authority, 'usually pulling up before we reached the outskirts of Bristol.' Still the horse flew walls, hedges and fences at such speed that his rider 'hardly knew when or if he had taken off'. Once or twice he hit an obstacle so hard that it stopped him dead, and Raoul was catapulted into the next field; but when he picked himself up Greyskin was always there, quietly cropping grass and looking at him as if to say, 'What's the matter with *you*?'

Friends kept saying, 'For God's sake don't ride that animal any more. He'll kill you.' And in the end they were almost proved right. The disaster happened in Jackaments Bottom, the start of Raoul's great hunt on Garland. The hounds were running hard and Raoul was galloping with the field when suddenly Greyskin put his foot in a hole, going so fast that he turned two complete forward somersaults. The local parson, who was riding behind, began mentally reciting the burial service, for when the horse came up for the first time, Raoul was still in the saddle, with his head perceptibly lower on his shoulders than before.

The American philanthropist and collector Paul Mellon, founder of the Mellon Collection in New York, winning the North Cotswold point-to-point – a picture painted for him and presented by the artist.

The horse survived unscathed, but Raoul remembered the ground coming up to meet him and nothing more. He was carried off unconscious on a gate, and in hospital it was discovered that he had broken a bone in his neck. He had also cracked one shoulder-blade and dislocated his back. The doctor put him in a stiff plaster collar, sat him in a wheelchair and told him he would never ride again – or do much else.

Two days later, unable to stand the claustrophobic feeling brought on by his rigid neck-brace, Raoul cut it off with a penknife and, although his head flopped around, he felt better. Then, by some strange chance, a friend whom he had not seen for years reappeared on the scene and took him to Bristol to visit an osteopath, a former boxer with cauliflower ears. When the man ran his fingers down Raoul's spine, he began muttering 'Oh, Lord!' and 'Good gracious!' At last he said, 'You're in a bad way, aren't you? Now listen to me: if you come to me twice a week for the next two months, I think I can get you well enough to enjoy life again. But I don't know about riding.'

His forecast proved accurate. He got the patient back on his feet, and in the course of the treatment the two men became good friends. Whenever Raoul gave him a cheque, the osteopath tore it up, so the only payment he received was in whisky and cigars. He died two years later, but Raoul remained eternally grateful to him.

The accident more or less ended Raoul's hunting career. He did go out a few times in 1938, but then he was forced to give up for good. In spite of this traumatic setback, the picture he painted of Greyskin after the war is wonderfully exuberant and romantic, with the horse prancing along beside its groom against a background of steep banks and ancient trees, and the artist's springer, Mira, frolicking in the foreground. One of the few pictures with which he felt reasonably pleased, it still hangs in his sitting room.

In the winter of 1936, when a period of hard frost made hunting impossible, Raoul went off to Kitzbühel, in the Austrian Alps, with his brother-in-law Ronald, an accomplished skier. In spite of his height, his high centre of gravity and the fact that in those days of few lifts he had to slog uphill for hours on skins attached to his edgeless skis, Raoul acquired a taste for winter sports, and the next year went out again, this time to Obergurgl. There he and Ronald narrowly escaped an avalanche, which wrecked their hotel.

Undaunted, they set out yet again in 1938, this time for Cortina, only to find the mountains unpleasantly tainted by Fascism. Not only did the daughter of the dictator Benito Mussolini arrive to open a new cable car; the hotel in which Raoul and Ronald stayed was full of Germans being chivvied about by jack-booted Gestapo. In the restaurant the radio blared out ceaseless Nazi propaganda, including interminable harangues from Hitler, and no German was allowed to start eating before these finished. The two Englishmen naturally ignored the prohibition, talking loudly and drinking their soup with exaggerated slurps, much to the fury of

the Gestapo, who searched their rooms and slit open the linings of their clothes in their search for incriminating documents. Compensation for such harassment came in the form of ten days' wonderful skiing on deserted slopes, but the experience was an unpleasant foretaste of what lay ahead.

'Going Down to the Start'. Raoul has always enjoyed watching horses race, but the sight of them in stables reminds him of human prisoners in Alcatraz, confined as they are to small boxes for twenty-three hours a day.

In 1939, with war looming, Raoul heard that the Army had started to commandeer all available horses, and he was faced with an agonising decision: whether to let his beloved old friends go to serve, perhaps in some horrible place like Egypt, or have them put down. With a heavy heart he chose the second course, and went to say goodbye. All five of them were out at grass in a field, Garland among them, and when they came galloping over to the gate to meet him, it was one of the most dreadful moments of his life.

ABOVE:
This powerful study of a stallion rearing may have been inspired by the stampede which Raoul witnessed in the mountains of southern Spain – see page 93.

RIGHT:
'On the Hill'. Mares and foals at rest were a favourite subject – and Raoul never painted a more comfortable group than this. The picture is one of relatively few that have remained in the family.

'Summer Morning' breathes with the freshness and warmth of May or early June, as low sunlight filters through the trees of an idyllic park.

Arab stallion. Raoul particularly admired Arab horses, with
their aristocratic looks: dished faces, large eyes, silky manes,
plumed tails and floating action.

CHAPTER SIX

WAR

When war broke out in September 1939, Raoul was almost thirty-eight, and still suffering from the after-effects of breaking his neck. Much as he would have liked to serve in the front line, his age and injury ensured that he had no chance of doing so.

At the outset of hostilities he was invited to raise a platoon of Local Defence Volunteers (LDVs), the forerunners of the Home Guard. His sole qualification was that he had once been a corporal in the Officers' Training Corps at Winchester; nevertheless, he managed to assemble about twenty farmers, their employees and friends for a never-to-be-forgotten first parade, which took place on the drive and in the stableyard at Farleaze.

In charge was a veteran regimental sergeant-major, a survivor of the First World War, and the volunteers brought along an amazing assortment of weapons, including two or three rusty shotguns, a scythe and several pitchforks. Once the RSM had got them fallen in, Raoul used his deer rifle to give a demonstration of how to slope arms, but in trying to copy his movements a man with a bill-hook overdid his enthusiasm and caught his neighbour a sharp blow on the ear. This produced an alarming flow of blood, and sent somebody scuttling for the first-aid kit.

As competence improved, the platoon began to challenge others in field exercises. It was announced that in one a secret message would be dropped by parachute at a certain point, and there would be a prize for the unit which first arrived at the site, seized the message and delivered it to headquarters. One of Raoul's brightest sparks was Corporal Jones, another veteran of the First World War. On the instructions of his commanding officer, he despatched some of his lads round the local pubs to find out where the dropping-point was to be. They ran the man who knew to earth in the Red Lion, and, by plying him with drink, wormed his secrets out of him. Armed with place, date and time of the drop, they were hiding in the best-sited ditches before the aircraft even came over, and they pounced on the message the moment it hit the ground, thereby earning the platoon a commendation from the pompous retired major who had thought up the scheme. Ridiculous as it

was in many ways, the Home Guard embodied a tremendous reserve of courage and determination, which would have seriously discomfited the Nazi invaders, had Hitler ever sent them in.

Even though he had no hope of serving in the front line, Raoul managed, by skilful manipulation of the old-boy network, to join a leading regiment. One day in 1940, on a traffic island in Piccadilly, he found himself alongside Major Archie Crabbe, a well-known character in the Scots Guards.

'What are you doing?' said Crabbe. 'Come and have lunch at White's.'

Along they went, and when Raoul explained that he could not pass a medical, Crabbe exclaimed, 'Oh, I'll fix that. I'll have a word with Colonel Bill and get him to see you next week.'

Bill Balfour, a small man with a high complexion, was Colonel of the Scots Guards. When Raoul marched into his office at regimental headquarters, the colonel was standing with his back to the visitor, hands crossed over his backside. Without turning or looking round, he said, 'Hullo. You Johnny's son?'

'Yes, Sir.'

'Bloody good fellow, Johnny. Best shot I've ever seen.'

'Yes, Sir.'

'Do a bit of painting, I understand.'

'Yes, Sir.'

'Go fox-hunting?'

'Yes, Sir.'

'Shooting?'

'Yes, Sir.'

'Fishing?'

'Yes, Sir.'

'Come Wednesday fortnight, then. Get yourself kitted out.'

The interview was over. The colonel had never turned round. So Raoul joined the Scots Guards, and found himself on the drill square at Pirbright, being yelled at by the regimental sergeant-major, who 'seemed to be impersonating a frustrated cock capercaillie.' Because he had kept fit by hunting and stalking, he was able to cope with the physical strain; but many fellow-recruits

LEFT:
Drum Corporal of the 9th Lancers: a picture painted to commemorate
Raoul's brother-in-law Ronald Macdonell, who commanded the regiment
from 1940 to 1942, and later was killed in action on the Coriano ridge in
Italy.

could not, even though most of them were young enough to have
been his sons, and by the end of the course there were only four
survivors, including himself and his friend Billy Fellowes, a
wonderful mimic and raconteur who later became the Queen's
agent at Sandringham, and with whom Raoul corresponded every
month for the rest of his life.

Because he had done so much shooting, he was detailed for, and
narrowly escaped, what might well have been a suicidal mission to
the far north. Somebody produced a wild scheme whereby a
private army of skiing snipers should go to Finland under the
command of Kermit Roosevelt, the drunken son of the American
president, to halt the advance of the Soviet Army with a few .303
rifles. Fortunately, at the last moment, the expedition was called
off. Instead, Raoul was put to teaching young officers straight from
school or from the City, and became, in succession, weapon
training officer, mortar officer, motorcycle instructor, lecturer on
Scots Guards history, map-reading instructor, fire officer and assis-
tant adjutant.

At Pirbright he met many cheerful characters, and some who
were less engaging – like the trick-cyclist who would come
wheeling into the Nissen hut at any hour of the day or night and
ride about the interior, keeping up a constant flow of anecdote
about recent events. The trouble was, the man was a kleptomaniac:
under cover of his frenetic movements and chatter, he would
collect up other people's belongings, which they had to retrieve
from his room next day.

The most popular form of sport – and in Raoul's view the most
dangerous game he ever played – was bicycle polo, which took
place on the unyielding asphalt of the drill square. For £10 apiece
the commanding officer's soldier-servant (a professional cycle-
maker in peacetime) ran up specially low-geared machines which
gave fierce acceleration, and as there were no rules, the cut and
thrust in inter-regimental matches sometimes became devastating.
With the commanding officer (who had only one leg) defending
the goal, and ruthlessly swiping junior officers off their machines
as they approached him, the four-man Scots Guards team carried
all before them and were awarded silver spoons.

The highlight of Raoul's war was his spell of duty guarding
Rudolf Hess, Hitler's deputy, who parachuted into Scotland on the
night of 10 May 1941 on what appeared to be a one-man peace
mission. After a brief period of incarceration in the Tower of
London, Hess was moved to Mytchett Place, a large Victorian
country house near Aldershot, which had been hastily fortified
with barbed wire and slit trenches, and was known for security

reasons as Camp Z. It was there that Raoul took command of the
guard, amid rumours that a force of Poles was preparing to storm
the place and execute the star prisoner.

Raoul was scarcely installed when who should arrive but
Brigadier Stewart Menzies, head of MI5. Before the war he had
lived at Sherston, only a few miles from Farleaze, and so knew
Raoul well. Now he seemed astonished, but also delighted, to see
an old friend, and at once said, 'Come and have a chat.'

Menzies confided that during Hess's stay in the Tower he had
been thoroughly interrogated by officers of MI5, but that he had
given away practically nothing. Now Menzies asked Raoul to have
as many meals with the prisoner as possible, to see if he could glean
any more information.

The exercise proved unrewarding. Hess spoke good English but
he seemed morose and hostile, and was evidently a practised
hypochondriac, constantly demanding medical attention and
refusing to eat the food set before him on the grounds that it was
poisoned. At one meal Raoul reached out across the table with his
fork, speared a piece of fish from the German's plate and ate it,
saying pompously, 'Herr Hess, I cannot believe that His Majesty's
Brigade of Guards would do anything so dastardly as to put poison
in your food.' The remark seemed to disconcert the prisoner for a
moment. He stared at Raoul as if sizing up the new commandant,
then leapt to his feet, clicked his heels, bowed and said, 'I apologise, Sir' – whereupon he sat down and finished his meal normally.

From that moment he conversed in an amicable way, and even
invited Raoul to stay with his family when the war was over; yet
there was always something strained about his manner. Like
everyone else at Mytchett, Raoul was well aware that a ban had
been imposed on photographing their prisoner. For reasons never
divulged, the Prime Minister, Winston Churchill, had decreed that
no picture was to be taken of Hess while he was in British hands.
So striking was Hess's appearance, however, that Raoul twice
persuaded him to sit for a pencil portrait – and powerful drawings
they proved, emphasising the subject's beetling brows and haunted,
deep-set eyes.

Raoul felt that Hess was basically a decent man who had had
the ill fortune to be caught up in Hitler's evil network. Equally, he
saw that his charge suffered from severe psychological disturbance,
and he was not surprised to hear that, after he himself had left
Mytchett, Hess jumped over the banisters, breaking a leg, and later
pushed a kitchen knife through a fold of skin on his chest,
pretending he had tried to stab himself in the heart. Although both
acts looked like attempts at suicide, the doctors diagnosed them at
hysterical efforts to attract attention.

Naturally Raoul longed to go abroad and, even if he could not
take part in the fighting, at least approach closer to the action. In
1943 it occurred to him that he might manage this without passing
a medical if he landed a job as a war artist. He was told to report

to the National Gallery for an interview with the director, Sir Kenneth Clark, who was then also in charge of home publicity. Along with three other hopefuls, one of whom had come all the way from Scotland, he arrived clutching a portfolio of his work, as instructed; but after an hour's wait, sitting on hard wooden chairs, all four were told that the director was too busy to see them, and they went away disappointed, uttering fearful imprecations.

With his photographic eye and mind and his ability to depict fast movement, Raoul would have made a splendid war artist. As it was, he produced few pictures with military subjects or connotations. One notable composition, however, was his portrait of the drum corporal of the 9th Lancers, which he painted after his brother-in-law, Colonel Ronald Macdonell, commanding officer of the regiment from 1940 to 1942, had been killed in action on the Coriano Ridge, in Italy, as second-in-command of the 2nd Armoured Brigade, in September 1944. Raoul gave the picture to the Lancers as a memorial.

Another dashing military portrait was that of Sergeant Fraser, hero of the action at Hougoumont Farm, during the Battle of Waterloo. For his 'special gallantry' in killing Colonel Cubières, commanding officer of the opposing cavalry, and in forcing shut the gate of the farmyard, the officers of the 2nd Battalion, the 3rd Guards, awarded Fraser a private medal. Raoul was moved by the fact that another Macdonell – also a colonel, and an ancestor of Clare and Ronald – was involved in the same action; he painted the picture of Fraser as a gift to the Scots Guards, and today it hangs in the commanding officer's changing room in the officers' mess of the 1st Battalion in Victoria Barracks, Windsor. A brilliant evocation of the action at Hougoumont, it catches tension and fear in Fraser's face and body, and arrogance in the attitude of the doomed cavalry officer as the point of the lance is about to be driven into his ribs.

During the war Raoul was given a month's special leave to paint two horses for King George VI. One was a filly which had won the Oaks, and the other Big Game, winner of the Two Thousand Guineas. When both pictures were finished, the artist was

Wartime sketch of Augustus John, who, as a visiting teacher at the Royal Academy Schools, helped shape Raoul's career. Although he often arrived the worse for drink, and went to sleep on his pupil's shoulder, John remained a lifelong friend.

summoned to meet the King at Buckingham Palace and spent an enjoyable hour chatting with him. As the King was another keen shooting man and had also been far up the Nile in the 1920s, they were not short of subjects for conversation; and Raoul delighted the monarch with his story of the evening when he was on guard from St James's Palace and challenged a nervous young sentry in the Buckingham Palace gardens. When he asked the guardsman what he would do if the door opened and the King came down the steps, the man looked horrified and said, 'I'd hide in f—— booshes, Sir!'

Later Raoul painted a second picture of Big Game for himself, and hung it over the mantelpiece of his flat in London. A frequent guest was Fay Compton, the actress and sister of the author Compton Mackenzie, and always, when she came to dinner, she stared at the painting in admiration – until at last, one evening, she asked if she could buy it. Knowing that she was hard up, in spite of her success in the theatre, and impelled by his usual irrepressible generosity, Raoul gave it to her. Years later she was obliged to sell it and now, after changing hands several times, it has come to rest in an ideal home, that of the celebrated jockey Willie Carson.

Another powerful wartime sketch was of the artist Augustus John, done in 1943, when the subject was sixty-five. Flowing white hair and gaunt cheeks make the sitter look older, and his eyes smoulder like those of an Old Testament prophet.

For much of the war Raoul was in London, enduring the blitz. He frequently had to extricate householders from the ruins of their homes, and was much moved by their fortitude. When he asked one old lady if she had anyone to look after her, she replied, 'Only my son, the coward; he's in North Africa with his regiment.'

Raoul's own luck held out to the end. On Sunday, 18 June 1944 he was supervising an exercise in Chiswick and lecturing a group

OPPOSITE:
Sergeant Fraser of the Third Guards, hero of the action at Hougoumont Farm during the Battle of Waterloo, kills the commander of the enemy cavalry, Colonel Cubières: a picture presented to the Scots Guards, in which Raoul served during the Second World War.

One of Raoul's few human portraits, this painting of Major Cuthbert Fitzherbert, a friend in the Coldstream Guards, done at Pirbright in 1943, struck the subject's son Nicholas as 'a brilliant likeness' of his father.

of Brigade of Guards officers on street-fighting. The bombardment by doodlebugs – V1 flying bombs – had started a few days earlier, and Londoners were struggling to accustom themselves to this unnerving new threat. From the ground they could hear the V1's rough-sounding engine, and people soon learned that, as long as the motor kept chugging on, they were relatively safe; it was when the sound cut out and the pilotless bomb began to dive, that one was in trouble.

That day, as Raoul put it, 'These horrible weapons were droning over like partridges, in thick fog, and mostly exploding to the north.' Then one was hit by anti-aircraft fire, which caused it to turn right: at 11.10 a.m. it plunged into the Guards' Chapel in Birdcage Walk, where it killed 121 of the people taking part in the Sunday service.

One of the next bombs brought down the building under which Raoul and his party were sheltering; several of them were blown over by the blast, but miraculously without any casualties. He vowed that, on the day when he finally met the Almighty, he would ask him why he 'chose them instead of us'.

Later he had another narrow escape, when he was detailed to supervise a demonstration of anti-tank mines in a part of Chiswick long since reduced to rubble. The reason he was chosen was that he knew the area well, because he and Billy Fellowes had established an agreeable routine of shooting partridges and the odd pheasant there on Saturday afternoons. As he remarked, among the boulders, heaps of rubble and deep holes, hordes of insects had 'literally gone to town', making the place a three-star restaurant for any game that had wandered in from the country.

The man laying on the demonstration was a highly efficient staff sergeant, well versed in explosives, and his aim was to initiate five or six senior officers of the Home Guard into the intricacies of the anti-tank mine. Raoul was just taking his seat in a pick-up truck to drive to the rendezvous when a clerk hurried out with a contrary order: he was to accompany the general to a street-fighting course in Notting Hill Gate. With some relief he set off in the opposite direction. Barely an hour later a despatch rider rushed up with a message for the general, who read it with a horrified expression, and handed it to Raoul. An anti-tank mine had exploded while the staff sergeant was fixing the detonator, killing him and most of the colonels.

Four days after hostilities had ended, Raoul suffered another severe loss with the death of his close friend Jerry Sheil, who had married Clare Macdonell's sister Dorrie. A tremendous horseman, Jerry had often hunted with the Beaufort before the war, and rose to become Commander, Royal Artillery, in the 51st Highland Division, only to drive over a mine when peace had come.

Raoul himself survived the war physically intact. Yet the upheaval of the conflict brought about a fundamental change in his life.

Raoul (right) and his friend Billy Fellowes look as though they have enjoyed a good lunch in the officers' mess at Pirbright. The two shot partridges together on bomb-sites in West London, and after the war maintained a lifelong correspondence.

Towards the end of the 1930s he and Clare had often entertained a glamorous couple, Erroll and Kay Prior-Palmer, who lived near Andover and several times went over to Farleaze for the weekend. The families were already connected by the fact that Erroll was a comrade-in-arms of Clare's brother, Ronald – both were regular officers in the 9th Lancers – and when the Prior-Palmers' daughter Karol was born in 1938, Ronald became her godfather. When Erroll played polo for England, Raoul wrote Kay a splendid letter about the occasion, embellished by a drawing.

At the outset of hostilities in 1939, Erroll went off to the war; the baby, Karol, was sent with a nanny to the relative safety of Wales, and Kay moved to London, where she drove ambulances. When Raoul was also posted to London in the Scots Guards, Clare made the grave mistake of asking Kay to look after him. This she did – with devastating effect.

Kay was then twenty-three, a strikingly beautiful young woman, red-haired and green-eyed and described as a cross between Ava Gardner and Rita Hayworth. Before the war Raoul's affection for her had been platonic but now the two fell in love, and Raoul never returned home.

Striking as she was in appearance, Kay was also well off and

exceptionally accomplished. She came from Shropshire – a member of the Bibby family, who lived at Hardwicke Hall and had made fortunes in shipping – and as a teenager she had trained for the ballet in Paris. In Raoul's view, 'she had an athletic elegance, and moved as if she walked on air'. In spite of severe short-sightedness she skied dashingly enough to win a medal in the Parsenn Derby at Davos, competing against professionals. She also rode beautifully, held a private pilot's licence and played the piano to concert standard. Once Raoul had fallen in love with such a paragon, there was no turning back and when he was invalided out of the army in 1945 with an intensification of problems caused by his neck injury, the two set up house together.

Looking back on his military career, he regretted that he had been granted no chance to distinguish himself, but hoped that by teaching 'a few good young men' to shoot and ride motorbikes, he had helped them survive the rigours of war.

Millais and Fellowes (left) in wartime pantomime gear, hamming it up in 'Treasure Island'. An outstanding mimic and raconteur, Fellowes later became the agent on the royal estate at Sandringham.

Raoul's drawing of his second wife Kay caught the exotic elements in her beauty. With her red hair and green eyes, she struck friends as looking like 'a cross between Ava Gardner and Rita Hayworth'. He called her 'Pussycat' or 'Pussul'.

CHAPTER SEVEN

SETTLING DOWN

After the war Raoul and Kay went to live at Oare, south of Marlborough, at the foot of the Downs. Clare, meanwhile, had sold Farleaze and moved to Ireland. Raoul never returned to her, but looked back on her as 'a saint completely dedicated to her Roman Catholic religion, and far too good for an agnostic like me'.

As racing and hunting picked up again after the war, he continued his career, although now he was commissioned to paint winning racehorses more often than hunters. In June 1946 the Derby returned to its proper home, Epsom, after a six-year exile in Newmarket, and the race was won by Airborne, a rangy, little-fancied grey which put in a storming finish to come home by a length at odds of 50–1. Asked to paint the horse by its owner, John Ferguson, Raoul placed it in one of his arcadian landscapes, with dark clouds swirling overhead.

He and Kay had set their hearts on finding a house in the Cotswolds, and in the winter of 1946–47, after months of searching, a friend rang up one evening to say, 'There's a total wreck near here going for a song. You'd better come and look at it.'

They arrived at Westcote Manor to find an ancient and beautiful stone house, part fifteenth-century, part eighteenth, in a state of advanced decay which had been accelerated by years of army occupation. Snow was drifting in through the roof, and the interior had been vandalised by the military, who had gone so far as to concrete in the fireplaces and had left the

To Raoul, Kay 'had an athletic elegance and moved as if she walked on air'. An accomplished skier, she also held a private pilot's licence and played the piano to concert standard. Her sudden death in 1985 left him devastated.

place festooned with signal cables. Outside, the garden had reverted to a hayfield, now full of dannart wire and empty gin and whisky bottles. The surrounding stone walls, once high, were mostly flat on the ground, and the whole property stood open to the four winds. Nevertheless, with it there came 120 acres of farmland and some fine trees, mainly elms and oaks – to say nothing of grand views out over the Heythrop country. Raoul and Kay fell for the place, bought it and set about imaginative restoration.

Dispensing with the services of an architect, Raoul himself made dozens of drawings and detailed plans and brought in a skilled local builder, alongside whom he worked for more than a year 'with great enthusiasm and harmony'. The builder produced an old stonemason who carved new mullions and lintels in his back yard. Having long fancied himself as a snapper-up of unconsidered trifles, Raoul was now in his element. On the floor of an outhouse in Warwickshire he found the studded wooden door of a former monastery, complete with its stone surround; taking it home, he made it his own front door. For £100 he bought an entire stone barn, complete with a sound roof, and used the material to extend the old house. He lined the front downstairs room with pine panelling bought from a friend who was an antique dealer. With the help of a former German prisoner-of-war, he rebuilt the garden walls and planted more than 3,000 trees, some of them in a covert at the bottom of

OPPOSITE RIGHT:
Sutton Place, home of the fifth Duke of Sutherland, who frequently invited Raoul to stalk deer on his forests in Scotland. Raoul painted the picture as a mark of gratitude. The house was later bought by the millionaire John Paul Getty.

a high, airy studio in an old tythe barn which stood in the stable-yard.

At this new base Raoul and Kay settled down in a state of mutual devotion. Because of his leonine looks, either Kay or her daughter Karol nicknamed Raoul 'Liony' – a name which has stuck to this day. He in turn called Kay 'Pussycat' or 'Pussul'. Some of his love and admiration show through in the fine drawing he did of her, which hints at the wild, slightly Bohemian streak in her character.

In his work he carried on as before, visiting owners and trainers, painting horses, giving pictures away. Now that he could no longer hunt, he generally went to Scotland to stalk in the autumn (see Chapter Nine), and made a winter pilgrimage to Davos or Klosters where Kay, an outstanding skier, was in her element.

Early in 1950, to their delight, Kay became pregnant, and at the end of October she gave birth to a son, Hesketh Merlin, always known as Hexie. The boy grew up at Westcote and had what he himself describes as an idyllic childhood. By the time he was ten, Raoul was already almost sixty; yet Hexie remembers him as an excellent father, playing tennis on the lawn and teaching him to shoot. In the studio the boy would watch his father painting, fascinated by the way he chain-smoked, with a cigarette permanently hanging from his lower lip and the ash curling over and over until inevitably it fell away. One ritual which Hexie always much enjoyed observing was the daily cleaning of the brushes, which took place after Raoul had had a cup of tea in the afternoon.

Among Raoul's racing friends was Fred Darling, the trainer; Raoul often stayed with him at Beckhampton, on the Wiltshire Downs, so that he would go out onto the gallops at dawn with the first string and make sketches. One of Darling's star performers, which Raoul painted, was Tudor Minstrel, winner of the Two Thousand Guineas in 1946, and the stable's leading jockey was the great Gordon Richards, a marvellous rider, but according to his boss, curiously vague about his mounts.

'He doesn't really know horses,' said Fred at dinner one evening.

'What do you mean?' Raoul asked.

'Gordon's a great jockey, and as straight a man as they come. But if I put him up on a four-year-old which would never win a bumper race, and told him it was my best prospect for the Derby, he'd never know the difference, provided the horse was the same colour.'

Early in the 1950s, Winston Churchill, once more Prime Minister after four years in opposition, wrote to Raoul saying that he had seen some of his pictures. Would the artist paint his own star performer, the grey colt Colonist II – and if he would take on

Raoul at Davos in the 1950s. After breaking his neck in 1937, he was forced to give up hunting. Instead he became an enthusiastic skier, and in spite of his height (6' 4") and his high centre of gravity, never sustained a serious injury.

the property designed to appeal to foxes. With Kay he planned an elaborate garden, divided up by yew hedges, with cypress trees as a background. Later, when he sold his childhood home, Compton's Brow, he brought up a pair of heavy wrought-iron gates from Horsham. Most important of all, he fashioned himself

the commission, how much would he charge?

Colonist II had been imported from France in 1949, and that year won three minor races, all on right-hand tracks (his jockey found he could not handle the left-hand bend at Lingfield). In 1950, much improved, he won eight good-class races: in 1951 he won the Winston Churchill and White Rose Stakes, and came second in the Ascot Gold Cup, earning the reputation of being every bit as tenacious a battler as his owner.

Fired by his record, Raoul replied that he would be delighted to paint the horse, but that he would prefer to do so free of charge. By return came a note saying, 'Dear Mr Millais, Thank you very much. Now virtue is its own reward, but art – no.'

When Raoul called at Churchill's house in Hyde Park Gate at 9.30 one morning, he found the Prime Minister sitting up in bed attended by several retainers, with a glass of brandy in one hand and a cigar in the other.

'Good morning, Mr Millais,' he began. 'You'll have a glass of brandy, won't you?' When Raoul declined, Churchill stared at him and said, 'Are you ill?'

'No, Sir, not at all. But I'm not as strong as you are.'

With that Churchill got out of bed chuckling, was helped into dressing gown and slippers and with the instruction 'Follow me' led his guest along a long, dark passage. At the end was a terrible picture of a black horse in a brown box. The light was so poor that Raoul could hardly see it, and when Churchill, looking round, barked, 'What do you think of that?' he hardly knew what to answer; it occurred to him that the artist might have been Winston's father, or even Winston himself. In the end he said, 'Not much, Sir.'

Churchill shot him another look and said, 'You're quite right. I only showed it to you for the size.'

While the painting of Colonist was in progress, Raoul twice visited No 10 Downing Street, and had long conversations on technique, the Dutch masters and other subjects. He found the Prime Minister extremely knowledgeable, and saw that he was a

It was Raoul's son Hugh who introduced him to bullfighting. Having spent two winters driving matadors around Mexico, Hugh became an aficionado, and when he bought a house in Spain, during the 1950s, he opened up a whole new vista for his father.

talented amateur artist. During one of the visits Churchill suddenly stared hard at Raoul and said, 'You see what's wrong with my painting, don't you?'

As he knew him fairly well by then, Raoul reckoned he would like a straight answer, and said, 'Yes, Sir. Of course. You've never had an opportunity to learn to draw or go to an art school.'

Churchill did not look very pleased. All the same, he said abruptly, 'You're quite right. No one has ever had the guts to say that to me before, but I know it's the trouble.'

The original painting of Colonist found favour with the horse's owner, so Raoul asked Churchill if he would mind if he did another one, with the Prime Minister in the picture. The answer was, 'Pray do – a very good idea.' Thus a second portrait of the horse came into being; the original is in the drawing-room at Chartwell, Churchill's former home in Kent (now a property of the National Trust), and the other in the Churchill Exhibition at Blenheim Palace.

Not all Raoul's commissions went smoothly. When Harold Coriat, Master of the Vale of White Horse Cricklade, asked him to paint his wife and children, Raoul did not realise that the family was in financial difficulties. They lived in some style in a manor house with the dire name of Twatley, near Malmesbury, and standards of maintenance were exceedingly high: there was a prize-winning herd of Guernseys and horses galore, the post-and-rail fences were freshly painted every year, and the 15-foot yew hedges round the outdoor *manège* were always immaculately clipped. Yet this façade was deceptive, for Coriat – known locally as 'Camel' – was notorious for never paying bills, and when a group of shop-

Supreme Court, with Charlie Elliott up, painted in 1955. After the Second World War, when Raoul received commissions to paint successful racehorses, trainers often received him with suspicion, until they realised how much he knew about his subject.

keepers in Malmesbury ganged up on him to refuse further credit, he was declared bankrupt. In fact there was plenty of money in the background, for Priscilla Coriat was heir to the furniture magnate Sir John Maple, but funds were not immediately available.

Before the war Raoul had lived within a few miles of Twatley but now, returning to the area from another country, he knew nothing of the family's circumstances. He was therefore happy to paint his principal subject, whom he described as 'a very nice woman, very handsome,' and her three daughters, two from her former marriage to the sixth Earl Howe, and one by her second husband. He set the family in one of his romantically Arcadian backgrounds, with Mrs Coriat seated on a garden bench, clad in a full-length white dress and flanked by the three girls and a huge stone urn poised high on a pillar. It seems ironic that two of the girls are with their ponies, for their mother hated horses and never rode – but that, no doubt, was what 'Camel' prescribed.

Although it was immediately judged a success, requests for payment of the £500 fee – a considerable sum in those days – went unanswered. Months later, Raoul mentioned the matter to a friend who, without telling him what he was doing, 'sent in the bailiffs, who started putting labels on all the furniture'. In due course the friend extracted the money, but Raoul was hideously embarrassed, because Mrs Coriat naturally thought that it was he who had sent the ferrets in.

Raoul's tendency to deprecate his own work remained incurable. When the Canadian millionaire Bud McDougal sent over his private jet to fetch a specially commissioned painting and then wrote to say that the picture had moved a young artist to tears, Raoul immediately wrote back saying, 'My God – I didn't think it was *that* bad.'

Mrs Coriat and her daughters: a successful and romantic family portrait from 1952, but one with a fraught background. Harold Coriat, who commissioned the picture, refused to pay for it, and was eventually declared bankrupt.

BELOW:
Raoul's lurcher Polly, a stalwart of the inter-war years at Farleaze.

RIGHT:
During the 1950s Raoul and Kay spent two summers at the Villa Malcontenta in Venice, and he considered this statue of the fifteenth-century general Bartolommeo Colleoni, by Andrea del Verrocchio, the best equestrian sculpture he had ever seen.

FAR RIGHT:
Rob Berkeley with the Berkeley hounds and the castle in the background. The picture, painted in 1969, was commissioned by members of the hunt and presented to the subject to commemorate his completion of forty years as Master.

Sleigh ride in Davos, perhaps Raoul's favourite ski resort. This painting has been used on numerous occasions as the design for charity Christmas cards.

OPPOSITE:
Premonition, one of the stars on the flat in 1953. The colt won several races, including the St Leger, and started as joint-favourite in the Epsom Derby, but was unplaced.

LEFT:
'Wild Horses'. An apocalyptic vision, set in mountains which look like the Sierras of southern Spain. Although Raoul painted relatively few dogs, he portrayed their anatomy and action as faithfully as those of horses.

BELOW:
Sketch of Nijinsky. First of the great sons of Northern Dancer – the most influential stallion of the past fifty years – Nijinsky was bred at E.P. Taylor's Windfields Farm in Canada and trained by Vincent O'Brien.

ABOVE:
Raoul painting at Westcote during the 1970s. He established his studio in a handsome old stone barn, decorated with many of the big game heads brought from his father's collection at Compton's Brow.

LEFT:
The astonishing Nijinsky, who in 1970 won the Triple Crown – the Two Thousand Guineas, the Derby and the St Leger. That year he also won the King George VI and Queen Elizabeth Stakes and the Irish Derby, but was narrowly beaten in the Prix de l'Arc de Triomphe. Raoul presented this picture to the National Horseracing Museum at Newmarket.

Racing at Newmarket. A departure from the artist's formal style of portraiture: in this fine action picture the suggestion of the horses' speed across the Heath is heightened by swirling movement in the cloud overhead.

OPPOSITE:
This Arab stallion belonged to Raoul himself. Years after painting it, he saw the picture hanging in a house in Wester Ross. The owner, asked why she had bought it, replied, 'When I die, that's the horse on which I'm going to heaven.'

Equine family life has always appealed strongly to Raoul, as in this calm, comfortable painting of a mare and her foal in idyllic sylvan surroundings.

El Serafin, the eighteenth-century smuggler's house overlooking the Straits of Gibraltar which Hugh and Suzy Millais restored during the 1950s and 1960s. Raoul loved combing breakers' yards for old doors, beams and other treasures.

CHAPTER EIGHT

SPAIN

For Raoul a new era opened in 1958. For some years Hugh and his wife Suzy had been living in Spain, renting a house at Los Bolices, near Marbella. After university in Mexico and work in Venezuela as an architect, Hugh spoke Spanish as well as he did English; he was also an expert on bull-fighting, for in Mexico he had spent two whole winters driving two leading matadors from one engagement to the next.

In 1957 Kay and Karol went out to Los Bolices for the summer, and Kay fell in love with Spain. Next year, Raoul accompanied her and when they heard that a friend, Ridian Crichton-Stuart, was proposing to sell an old house high on the south coast, above the Straits of Gibraltar, they hastened to go and look at it.

The place was named El Serafin ('The Seraph'), after the smuggler who built it, in about 1720, on a site that gave him commanding views of the Straits and of the traffic passing through. Raoul's first impressions were mixed. The track which twisted uphill towards it was exceedingly rough and scattered with large rocks. The entrance consisted of two stone pillars, with the remains of a brass bedstead sagging between them. 'Shades of the Emerald Isle,' he thought. But the air was hot and dry, and alive with the songs of nightingales and golden orioles, and the view was phenomenal. He got out of the car, removed the barricade, looked back at the view and as he returned said to Kay, 'Never mind what the house is like. This is it.'

When she saw the decrepit, ramshackle structure ahead of them, she burst into tears. 'I always knew you were slightly mad,' she sobbed, 'but this is too much.'

In fact it was – or became – perfect. The house was bought by Kay's family trust and Hugh and Suzy set about restoring it. They moved into what remained of a tower, a wing and a donkey stable, and recruited a team of local builders, who swung about their flimsy wooden scaffolding like acrobats. Now as never before, Raoul's magpie tendencies were given full rein. With Hugh he toured Andalucia snapping up 300-year-old doors, windows, panelling, ironwork grilles, oak beams and other treasures from breakers' yards, never paying more than the equivalent of £10 for any item. One of his favourite hunting-grounds was the flea market in Madrid, and under a sack in Seville he found a wonderful carved oak figure of St Francis.

The local workmen were not entirely *au fait* with modern plumbing practice: at one stage Hugh had boiling water in the lavatory and a stone-cold supply to the bath. The builders were also riddled with superstition: they insisted that a naked light bulb should burn day and night, and they kept a bullfinch in a cage to ward off evil spirits. Perhaps their intuition was not far wrong, for after the stable had been converted into a guesthouse with two double rooms, visitors who slept there sometimes complained that they had been awoken in the small hours by a donkey standing at the foot of their bed. Some nights, too, very odd noises came from the unoccupied top floor of the tower.

Along with the house the Millais tribe inherited a marvellous couple, Blas and Theresa, whom they found living in a shack with mud floors. Blas looked after the house and grounds and had, among other accomplishments, a unique method of dealing with the constant failures of the electricity supply. He would climb a ladder, seize a naked wire in either hand, wait till the current was restored and then, having received a healthy dose, shout '*Bueno!*' before returning to earth, not merely undamaged but, as he claimed, much stronger. Theresa cooked wonderful meals which were washed down by a powerful wine called Jumilia, known to the family as 'the red infuriator,' such was its effect on unwary guests.

The only other employee on the 15-acre property was known as 'the Maestro' – a skilled handyman, carpenter, stonemason and many other things beside. When Raoul brought out drawings and templates of an eighteenth-century balustrade he had found in Gloucestershire, the Maestro set about making moulds and casting new sections with such enthusiasm that he was with difficulty restrained from extending his master-work all the way down the drive to the coast.

In those days smuggling was still a major industry in the region. Fast motor launches brought cigarettes over from Tangiers in vast quantities; sometimes the police intercepted them, and the Millais household would hear machine-gun fire rattling up from the Straits. On land, dogs trained to recognise and avoid the green-uniformed Guardia slipped away at night into the high sierras carrying loaded panniers. On the other hand, it was legitimate and easy to go duty-free shopping in Gibraltar, where the amenities included large tins of caviar which the crews of Russian ships had exchanged for cheap shoes and clothes.

Years of improvement made El Serafin once again a magnificent house. Kay established a small but attractive garden, watered by a spring which rose at a point high up the mountain. A swimming pool, above the house and below the cork wood, which was also fed by the spring, gave endless entertainment to children of all ages – although care had to be taken to evict the adders which came up the overflow pipes. (After his experience of being forcibly ducked at prep school, Raoul never felt entirely at ease in the water).

To the main wall of the tower, which was white, he attached a bronze, Giacometti-like figure of St Michael, and when lit by a powerful bulb from below, this threw a large and impressive shadow. A fountain carved from rose marble graced the patio, and two cypress trees, planted one on either side, grew to a fine height. One February, after torrential rain – 80in. in ten days – these both blew down, but the family hauled them upright again with ropes and guyed them for several years until the roots had taken hold again. In contrast, a plan to make a fortune by growing avocados was washed out when more floods swept the five-year-old trees away.

The bird life was spectacular, for the house lay on the route of raptors migrating north from Africa in the spring and south again in autumn; in September hundred of eagles, kites, honey buzzards and lesser hawks would circle overhead, waiting for the right wind to carry them southwards. High up in the mountains behind, lammergeiers and eagles nested. Two owls lived in the forest at the back of the house, and at night Raoul often hooted them down into the *nogal* (walnut) tree by the patio.

Apart from a bull which insisted on taking its siesta on the drive and kept returning, even after being driven off with stones, the only real drawback to the place was the *Levante*, the wind which blew up from North Africa, bringing fog, damp and depression. Sometimes it continued for ten days at a stretch and sent the suicide rate soaring.

When Raoul first went to El Serafin, the Costa del Sol was blessedly unexploited. The road along the sea was no more than a pot-holed track which linked small fishing communities, and it was littered with smashed or burnt-out vehicles. Then, year by year, the beautiful coast was vandalised and ruined by the proliferation of hideous hotels and houses. Similarly, the golf course at Soto Grande, now world famous, was barely used when Raoul first knew it, but

OPPOSITE:
In the High Sierras. One of Raoul's most striking paintings, this sprang directly from a fantastic scene he witnessed in the mountains behind El Serafin, when a thunderstorm panicked a herd of horses and sent them charging in all directions.

millionaires' villas quickly sprang up all round it, and the pressure of demand led to the construction of a second course nearby.

For more than twenty years trips to El Serafin were an integral part of Raoul's life. Hugh and Suzy lived there all year round, and he and Kay would go out for a couple of months in spring, then again in autumn. Dozens of friends came to stay, and he looked back on that quarter of a century as 'a time of continual enjoyment.' Yet by far the most important result of his involvement in Spain was that it gave his work an entirely new direction.

It was Hugh, already well versed in the art, who introduced Raoul to bull-fighting, and suddenly, in his late fifties, he became an *aficionado*. When Hugh took him to his first *corrida*, Raoul warned him, 'If I see a horse hurt, I'll never come again.'

'You won't,' Hugh assured him, and he was proved right. In twenty-five years Raoul sometimes saw a horse knocked over but never one injured, largely because the picadors' mounts were by then protected by steel curtains round the body. What seized his imagination were the colours and the excitement of the arena, the panache of the participants and the drama of not knowing what the outcome of each contest would be. In a lyrical passage he described how, after the ritual, swaggering entrance of the matador and his entourage, salutes to *El Presidente*, and the ceremony of the keys, the flourishing of capes and roars from the crowd,

... an electric silence falls as the doors open and the first bull charges into the ring and skids to a halt. He comes from one of the most famous farms, with a pedigree going back generations. He has inherited his fine appearance from his father (they say), his courage from his mother. A roar bursts from the spectators as he looks round the ring, selecting a victim.

A matador advances, swinging his *capote* [cape], and makes several passes. He sees that this bull is 'on wheels' – one who charges straight: no hooker. The crowd roars again. The picador enters, mounted and with a lance – his function to break down the bull's neck muscles. Then come the bandilleros, who dance in to place their darts, with easy grace, but at great risk to themselves.

Silence falls again as the matador walks forward carrying his sword and the *muleta* [his stick with red cloth attached]. He executes one dangerous pass after another, with the crowd yelling 'Ole! Ole!' if they approve of his technique. In the end he despatches the bull with – he hopes – one thrust of his sword, and then is awarded the ears and tail. As he tours the ring to a further storm of applause, hats and wine bottles come flying into the arena.

The nearest ring – a large one, holding 14,000 spectators – was at Algeciras, only 5 km from El Serafin, and Hugh would book an *abono*, which gave tickets for the week-long *feria* every year. Elsewhere Raoul was often upset by cruelty to animals, but in the bullring it did not seem to worry him. He would sit absorbed by the spectacle, sketching furiously. To him the *corrida* was a beautiful art-form, and he often said that, if he were a bull, he would far rather die in the ring than in an abattoir.

Three *matadors* lead the procession into the bull ring: when the rest of the company has formed up behind them, they will take off their hats and make their formal bow to the president. After a show of Raoul's paintings and drawings in Marbella, the Spanish press hailed him as 'the new Goya'.

The wonderful quality of his work – the skill with which he caught the attitudes of the participants, the excitement and danger and dark beauty of bull-fighting – was strikingly confirmed when he held an exhibition of his drawings in Marbella. To his astonishment, every picture sold, and the Spanish press hailed him as 'the new Goya'. The eulogies were slightly spoiled by the fact that several newspapers printed a photograph of Hugh, rather than of the artist, which looked as if it had come from a 'wanted' poster. At least the mistake enabled Raoul to remain incognito, and to escape unwelcome publicity. Among the fan letters he received was one from a duchess who asked if he was a relation of Goya, whom she claimed to have known well. Goya had died in 1828, 130 years earlier, and Raoul, though initially flattered, later discovered that the lady was ninety-two years old and in care.

One day in the 1960s he and Kay were invited to lunch by American friends who entertained on a grand scale at their house near Malaga. To accept meant a drive of 100 miles each way, over dreadful roads, but they thought it worthwhile. Arriving rather late, they found at least twenty other guests already sitting at a long table in the open.

As they were apologising to their hosts, Raoul saw a grey-haired, grey-bearded man stand up and beckon to him from the far end of the table. He found that a place had been kept free, and as he came up the man said, 'I'm Ernest Hemingway. May we have a talk?'

Hemingway had been a friend of Hugh's for the past five years, and now he told Raoul how enormously he admired his father Johnny: 'I've read all his books, and he's like a god to me.' He said much the same of Frederick Courteney Selous, Raoul's godfather, and an hour vanished as the two talked big-game and bull-fighting. Raoul found Hemingway quite unlike the aggressive, bombastic character he had imagined from newspaper articles; he was exceedingly polite, his knowledge of big-game hunting was impressively thorough, and he numbered all the leading matadors of the day among his friends. Luckily Raoul had read most of his books, including his anthology of bull-fighting, *Death in the Afternoon*, so the conversation never flagged, and their neighbours did not get much attention.

Hemingway had been hoping to take over Johnny's entire collection of big-game heads, and he planned to build a museum in Iowa to house them. Whether or not he would ever have got permission to export so large a collection is another matter, but before he could bring the idea to fruition he discovered that he had diabetes of the brain, and in July 1961 he shot himself. Raoul felt he had lost a kindred spirit, and his father's heads had to be dispersed. Seven world-record specimens, including those of Raoul's giant sable antelope and ibex, found their way to the studio at Westcote, but the rest were scattered.

Besides many memorable bull-fighting drawings and paintings,

The celebrated *matador* Antonio Ordoñez studies the bull in the first *tercio* or stage of a fight in the ancient ring in Ronda. The *peon* whose cape is visible in the foreground has attracted the bull so that the *matador* can observe how he moves.

OPPOSITE:
A classic *pase de pecho*, or chest pass. Lying on the ground is the *montera*, or bullfighter's hat, which has been knocked off the head of one of the *peons* assisting the *matador*.

Spain also inspired one of his most striking horse pictures, *In the High Sierras*. Early one morning he set off from the house to climb to a lammergeier's nest and in the distance, as he looked towards Ronda, he saw a pall of dust hanging in the air. The sky was full of black clouds, and an occasional shaft of lightning, followed by a faraway rumble, warned that a thunderstorm was brewing. But the dust was not the result of any disturbance in the sky: as he sat on a rock and watched, he saw that it was being stirred up by the hoofs of a large herd of horses.

Presently he could see that they were being driven by two mounted men and their dogs, perhaps heading for some fair in the south. As they passed below him, he was able to count the loose horses, and found there were more than 150, proceeding in a relaxed group.

Then suddenly a lightning bolt exploded in their midst, instantly followed by a crash of thunder. Chaos followed. Terror-stricken stallions and mares bolted, neighing and scattering in every direction; some galloped away back towards the north, the direction from which they had come. Seconds later a deluge came hissing down, and Raoul took shelter in a shallow cave. When the rain eased

A *Miura* bull, from the Miura ranch, at the *feria* of Algeciras. These bulls have relatively poor legs but exaggerated *murillo*, the tremendous muscle on the shoulders, above the front legs – the trademark of the breed.

twenty minutes later, there was no sign of horses or men. By then the sun was up but the land, though wet, was empty. It was as if nothing had happened, or as if the whole stampede had been a dream. Yet the sight had been so apocalyptic that he later committed it to canvas, and he has always kept the picture, one of his favourites.

The most astonishing coincidence of Raoul's life occurred at El Serafin. After his mother's death in 1958 he went to sort out the contents of Compton's Brow, and in the attic found a collection of pictures stacked against a wall. Among them was a portrait of the Duke of Medinacelli, a Spanish grandee of the fifteenth century or earlier. In due course he took the picture to Spain and

hung it in the house there. One evening the Duchess of Lerma came to dinner, and when she saw the portrait she stopped dead.

'Where on earth did you get that?' she gasped.

Raoul explained, and asked what his guest knew about Medinacelli.

'He was the first duke, and my ancestor,' she said. 'He owned most of Andalucia, and all the land round here.'

By an extraordinary fluke, the Duke had come home at last.

93

RIGHT:
A *peon*, one of the *matador's* assistants, distracts the bull by flapping his cape.

Diego Puerta, a famous *torero* of the 1950s, performs a *media veronica*, or half sweep of the cape, in which the matador pulls the bull close round him by turning the folded cape tightly past his right hip.

The second *tercio* of the bullfight is the placing of the *banderillas*. The *banderilleros* call the bull to them, rise high on their toes, and drive in their darts. The infuriated bull responds by swishing his tail and tossing his head.

95

OPPOSITE:
Peons moving a bull so that the *matador* can assess its likely performance. He needs to pick up all the clues he can about how it behaves, which way it tends to hook, and whether it has a broken or a steady run.

One of Raoul's finest bullfighting pictures. The bull has knocked down a *picador* and his horse, and is trying to gore the man. Through the clouds of dust *peons* can be seen performing a *quite* – a manoeuvre designed to draw the bull away.

Having lured the bull close past him, by putting one leg out and whipping it in again, a *banderillero* leaps into the air before plunging his *banderillas* into the side of the shoulder muscles as it goes by.

ABOVE:
The bull at the start of the *corrida*. Having just come into the ring, he is electric with hostility, charging this way and that in search of something to attack.

RIGHT:
A bull going through the *matador's* first pass: he has just hurtled past the man and flicked his cape up in the air.

LEFT:
A *torero* attracts the attention of the bull by flicking his cape, which is cerise on one side, yellow on the other – the old colours of Spain, blood and sand.

ABOVE:
A *rejoneador*, an aristocratic *torero* who fights bulls from horseback in the antique manner, with a spear – a method still practised by a few experts today.

LEFT:
At the start of the third and final *tercio,* the *matador* Paco Camino sweeps off his hat to perform *el brindis*, the dedication of the bull to a selected person in the audience: possibly his girl friend, possibly the president, possibly another *torero*.

FAR LEFT:
A *peon* holds his cape at the ready as he awaits instructions from the *matador,* who communicates through the noise of the crowd by hand signals familiar to all the participants.

Johnny Millais sent this letter and sketch of advice to his son when Raoul made his first visit to the Scottish Highlands at the age of twelve. It seems curious that the expert big game hunter drew the point of aim so far back on the beast, over its belly rather than its heart.

CHAPTER NINE

IN THE HIGH HILLS

It was at Fealar, in Perthshire, that Raoul shot his first stag, in 1913. The forest then belonged to the Duke of Atholl, but it had been taken on a long lease by Raoul's great uncle Melville Gray (younger brother of his grandmother Effie). Fealar was – and remains – a grand, wild place. The lodge is the highest in Scotland, standing 1,700ft above sea level at the end of a 16-mile rutted track, and for a twelve-year-old boy the journey there was an adventure in itself.

'My Dear Raoul,' wrote his father from Compton's Brow on 10 September, 'Here is where to aim at the stag,' and he drew a little sketch of a rifle's sights centred on a stag's heart. 'Remember the rifle shoots about 9 inches above the tip of the white foresight. I am glad to hear you have arrived safely and hope by this time you are amongst the grouse and deer.'

Imagine Raoul's excitement when he was entrusted to the care of Davie Macdougall, stalker on the forest all his life. He never forgot how they crawled in towards a group of stags, with Davie hissing at him, 'Keep yer head doon, laddie, and yer backside as well!' When they reached a firing point some 75 yards from the beasts, the stalker shoved across the old .256 Mannlicher, with the urgent instruction, 'Mind the safety-catch!' Peering over the top of the mound, Raoul saw about ten stags, all with their heads up, staring straight at the intruders. 'The two on the right are worth a shot,' Davie murmured.

By then the boy was juddering so violently with stag fever that he had to make an all-out effort to hold the rifle steady. The foresight was 'dancing about like a mad mosquito'. When he fired, one of the stags dropped dead in its tracks, shot through the neck. As they hurried up to it, Davie cried, 'Well done! You got the heaviest of the lot!' and Raoul forebore to say that he had been aiming for the heart. It was a proud moment when the stalker slapped blood from the gralloch on his face, with the words, 'Dinna wash it off until tomorrow!'

The next year at Fealar, when he was only thirteen, Raoul had a still more stirring adventure. Old Geordie the shepherd told him that a big stag was coming over the march at dawn, and that it might be worth spending a night in a tumbledown bothy to get a chance at him at first light. In the evening, therefore, the lanky boy set off with rifle and blanket, to find that the bothy retained only part of its roof and that its walls had no mortar left between the stones. As he huddled in a corner, the north wind whistled through the crevices and he spent a wretched night; then, as dawn approached, he crept outside only to find everything shrouded in fog. Out of the mist came occasional roars, but because he could see nothing, he walked home disappointed.

That evening he set out again, better equipped, and passed a more comfortable night. Before dawn broke he heard occasional grunts and roars, and daylight revealed a big stag rounding up hinds on the near side of the march. The beast was close enough to make a fair target, but in his excitement Raoul placed his bullet slightly too far back, and the stag went away wounded into the neighbouring forest of Mar, which then belonged to the Duchess of Fife.

Running after it as fast as his spindly legs would carry him, he came out on top of a steep face and saw the stag lying below him. But also, much farther down, at the base of the hill, stood Mar Lodge, in full view. Knowing that he must finish off the wounded beast humanely, he killed it with another bullet through the neck. At the report, the lodge and its outbuildings erupted as stalkers, ghillies and footmen poured out; they spotted him at once, and began climbing towards him, letting out shouts and cries.

High above them, Raoul battled to remove the head from his stag, hacking at its neck with his pocket knife. In his haste he slashed his left hand, but at last he managed to free the trophy and swing it on to his shoulders. Galvanised by the commotion below, he struggled back over the march, with his rifle rattling against the antlers, and raced into the bothy, where he lay exhausted for several minutes. The head was a royal, and when his father saw it he said, 'Well done! But don't you ever shoot such a good head again. Always leave the best beasts on the forest.'

Fealar immediately became one of Raoul's happiest hunting grounds, for that same year, when he went to fish a pool below the

bridge on the River Tilt, he had outrageous luck. Wielding an ancient, borrowed greenheart rod, he hurled Jock Scot flies into the water 'like stones on the end of a string' and hooked no fewer than twelve fish. Nine broke the casts, but he landed three and bore them back in triumph to the lodge, where two expert fishermen abandoned stalking plans, went to the Tilt and flogged the water for the next two days without getting a touch. The boy was not entirely popular; and when Uncle Melville died at the age of almost 100, he left Raoul a stuffed pike in a glass case which had presided over the downstairs lavatory at his house near Perth – 'a well-deserved insult, perhaps'.

That breathtaking introduction to the Highlands launched Raoul into a lifetime of stalking, with what he called 'its golden moments and black disappointments'. The hunting instinct burned strongly in him, as it had in his father; yet, although he became highly skilled with a rifle, the shot was never the most important part of the operation for him, and he never went after trophies. Heeding his father's words, he always tried to select inferior beasts. The excitement lay in the challenge of approaching a truly wild quarry in magnificent surroundings, in using the wind and the ground intelligently, in crawling forward for a shot, belly to the rock or peat, with alert hinds ready to bolt and take the stag with them, or lying motionless for long periods, perhaps with legs immersed in an icy burn.

What Raoul loved was the nobility of the deer and their surroundings, and the subtle changes in the light as clouds floated their soft, grey shadows across the autumn hills. Again and again he captured the magic of the Highlands in his paintings. Unlike his celebrated Victorian predecessor Edwin Landseer, he hardly

Rear view of a red stag lying – a drawing which catches the grace of the animal's antlers, the solidity of its body, and its relaxed attitude in repose. It must have needed exceptional luck or skill to observe the stag from such close quarters.

Left:
Evening light strikes across old Caledonian pines on an island in Glen Affric, while clouds gather over the hills beyond, and a fish rises in the foreground: one of the many Highland scenes which remained etched in Raoul's memory.

ever took sketching or painting materials to the hill; rather, he would rely on his photographic eye and memory to recreate a scene in the studio, and he caught not only the characteristic attitudes of the deer but also the wonderful sense of space and distance that lends such enchantment to the Highlands. As one looks into his stalking pictures, one feels that one can see for miles. And never was evening light more hauntingly captured than in his painting of Glen Affric, in which low sunlight strikes through mist above a loch to illuminate the far side of the glen, and a single trout rises in the still water.

What he valued most of all was the company of the 'mountain men' – the stalkers and ghillies whose solitary calling seemed to enhance their natural manners, which were as perfect as his own. Treating them as equals, he loved spending days alone with them, hearing their stories, relishing their skill and knowledge, sharing the hardships of weather and terrain. He especially admired their toughness and self-sufficiency, and marvelled at the way they endured the Highland winters, often cut off by snow for days or weeks on end. Unlike most Sassenach stalkers, who go north only in the autumn, Raoul often drove up in winter to visit his friends. The trip itself could be a hazardous undertaking, but the stalkers were astonished and delighted to see him.

After the Second World War his stalking career received fresh impetus from a chance meeting in Surrey. He already had a slight acquaintance with Clare, wife of the fifth Duke of Sutherland – a tiny, frail-looking beauty known as 'the pocket Venus' – as he had met her out hunting with the Beaufort, and Kay knew her well. So one day the Millais were invited to lunch at Sutton Place, the Sutherlands' house near Guildford (later bought by the millionaire Paul Getty).

As usual, the place was boiling with guests, but somehow Raoul established a rapport with his strange, shy host. After lunch the Duke told him how greatly he admired his father. He said that he had all Johnny's books and asked Raoul to come and talk in his study alone. There he confessed that he had never before met most of the thirty-odd people he was entertaining, and that in general he found it hard to communicate or make friends. He described how, on his recent voyage from America, the *Queen Mary* had run into a storm, and how at the height of the gale one passenger had opened a porthole because he found the heat in his cabin oppressive. 'It slammed shut and knocked his head off,' said the Duke, adding as an afterthought, 'He was only a third-class passenger, of course.' In all the years of their acquaintance, Raoul could never decide whether the remark was supposed to be purely factual or intended as a joke.

The Duke also mentioned that he had a place in Scotland, and said that Raoul and Kay would be welcome to come up for as long as they liked in the autumn. So began a halcyon period of fifteen years in which Raoul stayed regularly at Dunrobin Castle, an immense Gothic fortress of grey granite sprouting from cliffs above the sea just north of Golspie, and went out to stalk on the huge forests which the Sutherland family then owned.

Fishing for salmon in the Brora, shooting partridges on the farms along the coast, walking up grouse on the higher ground and stalking over several hundred thousand acres – this, for Raoul, was paradise. Because the Duke himself was so half-hearted about field sports – he did not mind watching others fish for salmon, but could not himself bear casting – the stalkers and ghillies welcomed Raoul enthusiastically.

Soon he saw that in spite of his immense possessions, the Duke suffered from desperate insecurity, which he attempted to conceal behind a façade of arrogance. The glamorous and super-efficient Clare did all she could to help him, and in the north he had an able factor, or agent, who ran his vast estates. Wherever he went, he was surrounded by devoted servants. Yet he was unable to communicate properly with any of them and once said to Raoul, 'You're the only man I ever met I can talk to' – in Raoul's view one of the most pathetic statements he had ever heard. To him, the Duke was a man who had everything but also nothing; he lived 'in a world of luxury and isolated sadness'. In 1947, as a recompense for many kindnesses, he painted a fine picture of Sutton Place, with horses in the foregound and the house, ancient and sombre, behind, which he presented to his benefactor.

As all his employees knew, the Duke was liable to sudden whims. One evening he suddenly said, 'How many deer do you think there are on my forests? Would it be a good idea to get all the stalkers out to take a census?' Before Raoul had time to reply, the factor had been roused by telephone and told to set up a Scotland-wide count, during which every stalker was to walk his ground over the weekend and fill in a form showing the numbers. Of course they all stayed at home on the Sunday and compiled fictitious returns. When the Duke saw the numbers, he asked anxiously, 'Do you think there are too many?' To which Raoul replied, 'No – I think

OPPOSITE:
At the end of the day, two stags come home on Garron ponies. Raoul has always greatly admired the stalkers and ghillies who work in Highland forests, not least because their natural good manners so closely match his own.

it's just about right.'

Of all the Highlanders Raoul knew and loved, by far the most deferential was Murdo McLeod, head stalker on the magically remote forest of Loch Choire. As Raoul remembered, Murdo's politeness could become positively embarrassing. 'Would himself care to tak' the beastie on the left?' he would whisper after a long crawl. If an unseen hind jumped up and scattered the stags he would murmur, 'A calamitous affair, Sir! I must apologise. Would himself overlook the accident?' It was useless to assure Murdo that he was in no way to blame: nothing could erase the imagined blot on his professionalism.

Raoul's first encounter with Murdo was also his most memorable. The duke had sent him up to Loch Choire to stalk for an indefinite period, and when he reached the end of the eleven-mile gravel drive, there was the head stalker, hat in hand and a smile on his jolly red face, to welcome the new guest and make sure he was comfortably installed in the lodge.

After a cup of tea Murdo asked, 'Would himself care to come and see the boys?' Supposing that the stalker referred to his sons, Raoul readily agreed, and followed him through dark shrubbery towards a cottage. Some way short of the building, Murdo stopped and said, 'Would the Major kindly remain here behind this tree?' He then gave a low whistle and out of the cottage door came a woman in a long white dress, carrying a bowl in either hand.

To the newcomer, it was like a scene from *Macbeth*. The woman advanced a few steps, then began to sing in a high keening voice. As her lament floated away into the forest, out of the trees came two of the most beautiful stags that Raoul had ever seen: a royal with a perfectly shaped head and a wide ten-pointer. Both were nervous, and evidently sensed that there was something out of the ordinary about their feeding time.

Murdo and his visitor stood like statues behind their tree. Slowly the stags advanced, picking their way towards the pale figure, who held out their bowls towards them and continued her melancholy song. Then they began to eat but every few seconds they whipped up their heads and peered intently into the shadows in which the men were concealed. As soon as they had finished their supper, they turned and wandered away, disappearing back into the wood. Raoul found the experience deeply moving, especially when Murdo told him that he had found both beasts abandoned as calves on the hillside and had brought them home. His wife, who was 'not quite of this world', had reared them on bottles, and they had become her children.

The other stalkers on the Sutherland estate were fond of Murdo,

OPPOSITE:
Three stags graze by a Highland burn. On his many forays to the Highlands
Raoul hardly ever made sketches, but used his photographic memory to
reproduce details of scenes he had witnessed and to evoke the feel of the
rugged, large-scale landscape.

but they also liked pulling his leg. One day Hugh McKay, the head stalker from Dunrobin, took Raoul to the head of Loch Choire in a boat, and the two worked their way back towards the lodge along the forest's eastern ridges. The day was a glorious one and Raoul was far too engrossed by its ever-changing beauty to worry about whether or not he would get a shot. Hugh, however, was disappointed by the lack of shootable stags, and it was only when they came to the steep face above the lodge that they at last spied a pair of worthwhile targets.

There, a short way below them, were two stags with good bodies but poor heads: ideal beasts to cull. After crawling in, Raoul killed them both, right and left. Hugh was delighted, and exclaimed, 'Watch this now! We'll have a bit of fun with Murdo. He'll have heard the shots, right enough.'

Having dragged both beasts to the pony path, they left them concealed in some bracken and walked on down. As they approached the stalker's cottage, Murdo came running out to meet them.

Hugh pulled a long face and sighed. 'Bad news, Murdo. We made a fearful mistake and shot your boys.'

Poor Murdo! The colour drained from his face, and he stumbled away towards his cottage door. Hugh was shaking with laughter, but Raoul suddenly realised that the stalker was about to break the news to his wife, and that this could not be allowed to happen.

'Murdo!' he yelled. 'Stop! Come back! It's only a joke. We shot a couple of switches.'

The stalker stopped, turned slowly round, stared – and then took a rush at Hugh, who made himself scarce with some alacrity. It was several days before Murdo forgave him.

Another year Raoul was out with Hugh McKay in Dunrobin Glen on a hot, thundery day. They got a quick shot at a stag as it walked over a ridge, but were not sure whether or not the beast had been hit. As they ran over the top, there was the stag, lying on its back with all four feet in the air.

'That was a bit of luck,' said Raoul.

'Never mind!' Hugh told him. 'You did fine. If ye'd no taken him then, he'd never have given you another chance.'

Preparing for the gralloch, they took off their jackets and laid them on the ground beside the rifle, which Raoul had already unloaded. The stag was lying with one horn in a hollow beside a rock, and as Hugh drew out his knife he said, 'We need to pull him round. D'you mind taking a horn, while I take a leg?'

Raoul grabbed the upper horn and gave it a firm tug – where-upon the beast erupted into life with such violence that he was tossed into the air and landed several feet away. Hugh was flung on to his back, and the knife flew out of his hand. Looking up winded and bewildered, Raoul saw the stag trotting off as though nothing had happened. With a mighty effort he pulled himself together, ran across, grabbed the rifle, fumbled a couple of cartridges into the magazine and felled the stag, which had stopped broadside on, with a heart shot.

'Never saw the like of it,' gasped Hugh as he picked himself up. 'Your first bullet must have creased him across the top of the spine.'

Sure enough, they found a burn-mark across the stag's withers. and realised that the animal had been temporarily paralysed by the blow on its spinal cord as the bullet nipped its back. They also realised how phenomenally strong it had been to throw two large men to the ground.

Occasionally Raoul fell in with a stalker who seemed less than enthusiastic about his job, and this seemed to have happened one day at Conaglen, a grand forest bordering Loch Linnhe, opposite Fort William. The place was then owned by Raoul's friend Michael Mason, who sent him round to the far end of the ground, on the shore of Loch Shiel, to go out with Andy, a young stalker there.

Arriving by Land Rover at the boathouse, Raoul was met by a hefty young fellow whose face wore a dour look, as if he resented this intrusion onto his beat. Raoul's 'Good morning. You'll be Andy', received no more than 'I am that' in reponse, and the pair boarded a fibreglass boat without another word.

After a short voyage down the loch they pulled into the left-hand shore, landed on a shingle beach and set out to climb a precipitous gully full of loose shale, which made the going treacherous. When at last they struggled out onto the lip of a small corrie, they looked across to the grass slope on the opposite face and saw that it was crawling with stags.

'Some pretty good beasts there,' said Andy as he spied them through his telescope. Then suddenly he let out a loud exclamation. 'Good God! Look at that!'

Over the far skyline had come a perfectly inmense stag. His body was so massive that it made his legs appear very short. Instinctively Raoul said, 'He looks like a dachshund with a Christmas tree on his head', and to his amazement, the hitherto-sullen Andy began to shake with laughter. 'Verra guid!' he gasped. 'Verra guid!'

Once Raoul's observation had broken the ice, the stalker became more and more animated. 'I've heard talk of yon beastie,' he said. 'He's been seen down in the Forestry Commission ground. He must weigh twenty-four stone, at least.'

The stag came downhill towards them at a steady trot, heading for the herd below him. As he reached them, he broke into a lumbering gallop and charged in among his rivals, slashing with his antlers to left and right. The lesser stags scattered, and soon the whole face was teeming like a disturbed anthill. But hardly had the stalkers decided to try for the monster when he took off, back over the hill.

'They're terrible restless,' said Andy, watching the mass of stags as they seethed about. 'We might as well take our piece till we see what they're going to do.'

The two men sat down to eat their sandwiches, but they had hardly started when Andy cried, 'They're away! They're making for the pass! Run, Sir, run!'

They ran until Raoul's lungs were bursting, up and up, over ridge after ridge, occasionally falling, always charging on. At last they flung themselves down on a huge rock. Below them, in a deep defile, the stags were picking their way up through the stones in single file, moving slowly enough for the men to check them, one by one. Raoul, the painter, found the scene of riveting interest. As he recalled later, his artist's eye was 'attuned to notice colour, action, atmosphere, background, the fleeting moment when an animal shows fear, surprise or excitement'. He became so absorbed in watching the ascending cavalcade that he jumped when Andy clutched his arm.

'There's twa guid-bodied beasts coming up below yon black rock,' the stalker whispered. 'Big stags, but only fair heads. Tak' both of them if ye can.'

The shots, a right and left, were easy, but in the rocky confines of the gully they produced an astonishing effect. The two dead beasts rolled down into a group at least fifty strong, which exploded like a star-shell. Suddenly there were stags going in all directions; three or four bolted past within 10 yards of the prostrate men, their hoofs rattling over the stones. When the whole lot had gone, the stalkers collected up their kit and went down to gralloch their beasts, which were lying together in a deep, rocky cleft. Extracting them proved no easy task, and by the time they were safely in the boat, the day had turned into something of an epic. In the larder, one stag weighed out at over 18 stone, the other over 17; even so, according to Andy, they would both have 'looked like roe-bucks beside yon monster'.

Raoul said goodbye and thanked him. Then, as he was crossing to the Land Rover, Andy called out, ''Twas a grand day we had, Sir. I never saw the like of it. Will ye manage to come again?'

On another forest, Loch Luichart, Raoul one day got a stag early, and was on his way home with the head stalker. Dropping down towards the road to eat their sandwiches, they were about to settle in the sun on the back of a heathery knoll when Raoul saw, about 50 yards away, the tip of an antler showing over the top of a mound. He whispered to the stalker, and they both crawled in without the rifle. As they peered over the mound, there, facing away from them, lay a huge stag with the finest head Raoul had ever seen in Scotland – a fourteen-pointer, an imperial, with thick, black horns, long brow-points and four white points on top, each side perfectly matched.

'Ye'd just as well shoot him,' the stalker whispered, 'or else the poachers will get him.' But Raoul, mindful of what his father had told him years before, and remembering conversations with his host about trophy-hunting tenants who cared nothing for the good of the forest, declined to bag the monarch.

'Och well,' said the stalker, 'you can leave him if you wish. But we'll no see the like of him again.'

Sure enough, that majestic head was found next winter, cut off and abandoned on the roadside, along with the heads of two younger stags. Poachers had gunned them down in the headlights of their car and carried off the bodies for sale in Glasgow or Aberdeen. The men were later caught by the police, but the city magistrates, who in Raoul's view 'had never been farther afield than a picnic in the Trossachs', fined them a derisory amount and left them free to continue their murderous raids.

In the course of his long stalking career Raoul found that many places in the Highlands, if not positively haunted, had a sinister feel about them, and none more so than an old birch wood beside a strip of dark water known as the Black Loch, hidden away in the southern fastnesses of Loch Choire. On a hot, heavy day one September he and Duncan, an old stalker with a game leg, worked their way along the ridge towards the Dalnessie march at the southern end of the forest. Far below them on their left lay the Black Loch, cradled on all sides by steeply falling slopes, and the wood grew on a strip of flat ground along its shore.

Presently they spied three stags feeding in a corrie beneath them. Two had good heads, but when the third, a six-pointer, moved forward, they saw that it had a broken front leg. Because it was still in good condition, they reckoned that it must have sustained the wound, either from a bullet or in a fall, within the past few days and they decided to go for it.

As they moved off, an eagle soared out over the ridge and began to quarter the ground in the corrie. Three heads came up with a jerk. The two sound stags – a royal and an eight-pointer – set off at a fast trot in the direction of the march, but the lame beast started to hobble straight down towards the loch.

'Ay, it's the wood he's making for,' said Duncan. 'That's where the wounded stags go. I've never been doon there myself, but they say it's an awful queer place.'

Raoul immediately volunteered to run down and cut the beast off, telling Duncan not to come because of his weak leg, and saying he would rejoin him at the boat. With that he set off alone on a perilous descent, leaping down runs of loose shale in the floors of gullies and setting off minor avalanches. The lower he went the hotter the air became, and as he stopped for a moment, pouring with sweat, he was just in time to see the lame stag disappear into the trees.

More slithering and sliding brought him to the edge of the

forest, but the nearer he came to the wood, the stranger it seemed to be. Its floor consisted of great mounds with coarse grass sprouting from their tops, and in amongst the trees darkness prevailed. Hundreds of dead birches had fallen over and were

'The Fall'. In this allegory of the Highland scene Raoul portrayed Scotland's three most exciting species – a stag, a salmon and a golden eagle – even though the chances of seeing all three together must be millions to one against.

111

propped at angles on the branches of living trees. Among them were gnarled and ancient withies, many of which had given up reaching for the light and turned back towards the ground.

Through this grotesque thicket Raoul began to force his way. When he stopped to listen, all he could hear was a raven croaking its way over the Black Loch. Soon he became oppressed by a feeling of unreality and menace, which bore in on him more and more heavily the further he went. He also realised that he had very little chance of seeing the lame stag again; for one thing he was making too much noise, and for another visibility was extremely poor.

He decided to go on for another 100 yards and had just taken the first few steps when he heard a twig crack. He stopped. All round him ancient stags were rising from the ground. Against the dark background, they looked almost white; all seemed to be in the final stages of emaciation. The ghost-like apparitions made no attempt to move away, but stood staring as if he were a being from another planet. There must have been ten of them watching him, some only a few yards off.

What to do? Raoul decided to finish off as many as possible to put them out of their misery. Slowly raising his rifle, he shot three which looked to be in the final stages of decrepitude. In spite of the noise, the others did not move for several seconds. Then they began to drift into the gloom, and Raoul could not bring himself to kill any more.

Having unloaded the rifle and put it down, he approached the nearest body. To his amazement, he found he could lift the carcase with ease; it was no more than 'a bag of bones covered with what looked like hairy parchment'. The other two were the same, with scarcely an ounce of flesh on them.

Leaving them where they lay, he set off for the forest edge. On the way he passed two skeletons, the bones picked clean and shining white against the black soil.

Duncan was waiting by the boat. 'You look as though you've seen a ghost, Sir,' he said.

'You're right,' Raoul replied. 'I saw ten.'

The old man listened closely as he heard the story. Then he said, 'Ay, I've heard some strange tales of yon place. I wud nae gang in there for choice.'

In later years Raoul often wondered what happened to Murdo McLeod's two 'boys'; but he liked to think that in the end they joined their brethren in the birch forest by the Black Loch and that poor Mrs Murdo, who died soon after he had seen her, sometimes went there to cherish them with her food bowls and her mournful song.

Always closely associated with deer, in Raoul's mind, are grouse. He first shot grouse at Fealar when, at the age of twelve, he was sent out down the track from the high-lying lodge to get a bird for the pot with his .22 rifle. Ever since then he has been fascinated by the behaviour of this enigmatic species. His father once told him that the grouse was a 'mystery bird' whose secrets no human could unlock, and Raoul remains convinced that, in spite of much latter-day research, we still do not understand it.

In common with most people who shoot grouse, Raoul was often astonished by the violent fluctuation in numbers. One of the most amazing years in Scotland was 1921. Invited to shoot at Tomatin, he found himself in pole position for the last drive. He was using his grandfather's non-ejector gun, but even so shot forty-seven birds before the main drive started, as the beaters worked away from the line in a horseshoe formation. Then, to his dismay, the brass rim became detached from one of his cartridges, which jammed in the breech so that he could not close the gun. For the next half hour clouds of grouse poured over him unscathed, and shouts from the adjoining butts, occupied by men old enough to be his father, 'only exaggerated the nightmare'. Afterwards he reckoned that anyone with a properly functioning weapon who could shoot at all must have killed over 100 birds at that drive.

At Fealar, in his youth, there were practically no grouse. As he put it, 'If you walked all day on the flats above the lodge, you would be lucky to get a brace and a half.' But then one evening in 1919, as he was coming home with the stalker, his companion suddenly exclaimed 'My God! Look at that.' To the south the sky was black with thousands of grouse pouring in to settle on the flats. Raoul's Uncle Melville maintained a strict rule that no shotguns should be used after the middle of September, as the noise might disturb the deer; but by the end of dinner that evening the rest of the party had persuaded him to make an exception. In the morning four of them went out and shot 110 brace. Next day, the grouse had vanished to the north. Where had they gone? Where had they come from? What had set them off in the first place?

Later, in the 1950s, Raoul heard of another mass migration, this time in Sutherland. Hugh McKay told him how, one day in January, there had been a force-10 gale blowing from the west. Deep snow covered the land, but countless thousands of grouse packed in to blacken the slopes of eastern-facing hills. Then, as Hugh watched, to his horror he saw the whole lot lift off in a mighty cloud, which was swept out over the North Sea. Were the birds starving? Or were they driven, like lemmings, by some instinct to return home? And, once again, where had they come from?

OPPOSITE:
Autumn in the Highlands: a stag roars out his challenge to an intruder during the rut. An outstanding rifle shot, Raoul combined admiration for the deer with a clear understanding of the need to cull the herd selectively.

Stags in the snow. Unlike most amateur riflemen, who visit the Highlands only in the autumn, Raoul several times made the hazardous journey to the far north in winter, and was much moved by the fortitude of the professional stalkers.

OPPOSITE:

Stags coming up out of a steep corrie: a picture which perhaps carries echoes of the action sequence on the high ground in the north-east corner of Conaglen forest, in Inverness-shire, described on pages 109 and 110.

OPPOSITE:
Autumn colours in Sutherland. Seldom has an artist so well conveyed the idea of distance in the Scottish hills. Here patches of light and shadow draw the eye past the deer in the foreground to the far ridges and away into the sky.

Two stags lock in combat during the rut, while a harem of hinds hovers excitedly in the background. Raoul witnessed many such fights in the course of his stalking career, and brilliantly caught the tension of the occasion.

117

The use of Garron ponies to bring home the stags gave the artist a chance to combine two of his favourite subjects: horses and deer. As always, details of the harness, and the way in which the stags have been loaded, are meticulously correct.

OPPOSITE:
Half seen over a ridge, a stag throws back his head to roar during the rut – a painting that evokes the evanescent nature of Highland deer. The hinds have spotted an intruder, and in a moment will vanish into the mist down the corrie.

'The Sanctuary'. Stags lie and graze at their ease in a high, rocky glen. Many forests include a remote and inaccessible area of this kind, which is left alone because dead beasts cannot be extracted from it. The deer seem to know that in such places they are safe.

Red deer studies. Raoul
made hundreds of sketches,
always seeing to capture the
attitudes and movements of
the quarry which he
pursued so enthusiastically
with pencil, brush and rifle.

Black and white stallions fighting – a picture painted when Raoul was eighty-four. How many artists half that age could produce a composition bursting with such wildness, life and vigour?

CHAPTER TEN

LIFE AT WESTCOTE

In spite of steadily increasing renown, Raoul remained reck-lessly generous. One businessman, visiting his studio, took a liking to a particular picture and asked how much it was. The painting was one which he did not wish to sell, so he said, 'A hundred thousand pounds.'

'That's a bit steep,' said the visitor.

'All right, then. Ninety-nine thousand.'

At that, both men began to laugh, but on an impulse Raoul handed the picture over for nothing, and the man left 'with the lasting impression that all artists are certifiable lunatics'. Yet the exchange gave Raoul far more pleasure than the prospective buyer, even though he had gained a painting free.

By the 1960s Raoul's fame had spread to France, and he went there to paint several pictures for Prince Aly Khan, who delighted him by putting aside a special room to hang them in. Less engaging by far was François Dupré, a millionaire who, unknown to Raoul, had married the daughter of Hermann Göring and collaborated with the Nazis. He owned the Georges V hotel in Paris, several large hostelries in Canada and a stud farm in Normandy. There he was loathed by his employees, especially his stud groom, with whom Raoul made friends. The groom regaled Raoul with horri-fying stories of Dupré's collaboration, and, when he left, gave him a bottle of Calvados which he had buried in his garden in 1943 to preserve it from the enemy. Raoul still has it, unopened. Looking back years later, he reflected that in all his long career he had met only two really unpleasant characters – Dupré and the man who demanded to have stands included in his picture – and he has always felt guilty that, in his ignorance, he accepted commissions from them.

Celebrated visitors continued to call at Westcote, among them the Greek shipping magnate Stavros Niarchos, who arrived one day with a male secretary in a chauffeur-driven Rolls-Royce. In the studio the secretary ostentatiously brought out a cheque-book and laid it open on a table. After looking round for a few minutes Niarchos said, 'Mr Millais, you are a very good painter.'

'Thank you,' replied Raoul.

'Do you ever sell pictures?'

'Sometimes.'

'In that case, I'd like these.' Niarchos pointed at one wall on which were hung Raoul's ten favourites, none of which he had any intention of selling.

'Mr Niarchos,' he said. 'The trouble with you is you haven't got enough money.'

Raoul thought the Greek was going to knife him, he seemed so chagrined. The secretary looked as though he was about to pass out. But he put the cheque-book back into his pocket and the party walked outside. In the yard Niarchos recovered enough to apologise. 'I'm so sorry,' he declared. 'That's the best thing anyone's ever said to me.'

Raoul loathed rudeness or self-importance. One day in London he came across his old tutor and friend Augustus John, by then at an advanced age but trailing the latest of countless female admirers, the leading Italian sculptress Madame Fiori, a woman of large and powerful build. The lunch party went reasonably well until she turned to Raoul and said, 'Yes, Mr Meelay, I will sculpt you provided you shave off your reedeeculous cavalry moustache' – to which Raoul replied, 'I'll be delighted to, Madame, provided you do the same.' Deep frost settled on the gathering.

Like Raoul's mother, Kay was immensely sociable and loved giving parties (among other gifts, she had a brilliant knack of arranging flowers). Raoul was quite happy if she invited friends to bridge or dinner at Westcote, but he hated going to London, and frequently developed a migraine if threatened with an outing. He had a particular dread of grand cocktail parties, wherever they took place; if ever he was forced to go to one, his favourite trick was to pick up a bottle and circulate with it, pretending he was a waiter, so that he could not be cornered by bores.

He also pretended to hate actors, but of course he got on perfectly well with some, not least David Niven, who became a good friend. He delighted to tell the story of how the star once invited him to the première of his latest film in Leicester Square. As they arrived, Raoul was horrified to see that they had to approach the cinema through ranks of screaming teenage fans. Niven parried demands for a kiss and signed a few autographs with his usual suavity. Then Raoul saw a girl pointing at him and heard her say, 'Who's he, then?'

'Only some old bodyguard,' came the reply.

When Raoul told Niven, he doubled up with laughter and said, 'About time you knew your place.'

At Westcote Raoul's affinity with animals found new expression with the arrival of Bessie, a sow badger which had been dug out of a nearby sett. Raoul described her as 'a very small person who hated dogs and yet terrified them'. He installed her in the old saddle-room, which had a stone-flagged floor, and gave her the run of the garden. In summer, if he lay down on the lawn, she would climb onto his stomach and go to sleep; but under a full moon in winter she became a different creature, leaping up and down as she invited him to play hide-and-seek. During those wild games she always hid under the same bush, and if he went past, she set up a frantic whistling to call him back. Hexie also used to play with her, an elaborate game in which she hid a stick with a red blob on the end and made him search for it. When Raoul took her for walks through the surrounding fields, he taught her to search under stones for worms and beetles.

In the end he released her into the wide world, but still she came back for treats of bread and milk. Reflecting on how badgers live in civilised communities, 'and have a code of hygiene second to none', Raoul reckoned that they seem to 'have a long historical pedigree which has kept them apart from the rest of the animal world'. He concluded that 'badgers are not like other people, and surely belong to the Upper Sett'.

The older Raoul grew, the stronger became his feeling for the family. He was delighted to have Hugh and Suzy living for a while in the Dower House, a smaller building only a few yards behind Westcote Manor. In 1964 he was equally thrilled when his step-daughter, the beautiful Karol Prior-Palmer, married Simon

Raoul's step-daughter Karol Prior-Palmer, who in 1964 married Simon Maxwell and came to live in the Dower House at Westcote, less than a hundred yards from the Manor.

Maxwell and took over the Dower House, which they later rebuilt into a substantial dwelling.

In 1970 an extraordinary stroke of good fortune befell Hexie. For all his adult life Raoul had fascinated women, and few were more besotted about him than Jane McBryde, who raised horses, cattle and sheep in Herefordshire and owned a marvellous house called Dippersmoor, part stone, part half-timbered brick, dating from the sixteenth century and perched on an abrupt knoll above the village of Kilpeck.

Jane's father had been a close friend of M.R. James, Provost of Eton College and author of hair-raising ghost stories. Monty James enjoyed staying at Dippersmoor; with its timbered ceilings and dark-panelled walls, the place had a comfortable yet spooky air which suited him admirably, and he did much of his writing while on holiday there. But Jane's father died soon after she was born, and James became her guardian.

During the 1930s Jane often went over to hunt with the Beaufort and became obsessed by Raoul, who returned her affection but in a purely platonic way. Over the years Jane had relationships with many men, yet in the view of her Herefordshire neighbour and life-long friend Lady Mary Clive, they were all like schoolgirl crushes, and none was ever consummated. It seemed to Lady Mary that 'Raoul was always No 1 in Jane's life'. Certainly Jane was one of the staunch friends to whom Raoul's shift from Farleaze to Westcote made no difference. Her affection remained undiminished and when Hexie was born, Raoul asked her to become the boy's godmother. She was glad to accept, and as a young man Hexie often stayed with her in Herefordshire, helping out on the farm.

Then, towards the end of the 1960s, Jane fell ill. Aware that she was dying, she offered to leave Raoul her house and land but he said that he had a perfectly good house anyway, and after discussion they agreed that Dippersmoor should go to Hexie. So it did, on Jane's death in 1970, together with all its contents, which

Her Majesty Queen Elizabeth II arrives on Ascot racecourse in the state carriage after the ceremonial drive from Windsor Great Park: a picture commissioned to mark the Queen's silver jubilee in 1977. Raoul painted two versions.

included a splendid library and, tucked away in the attic, a drawing by Constable. But as the young man was only nineteen, and about to join the Army, Raoul made holding arrangements on his behalf, and installed as tenants the theatre critic Milton Shulman and his wife Drusilla. So, for eleven years, the Shulmans held the fort at Dippersmoor, and when Hexie finished his term in the 10th Royal

Hussars he took over from them, making the place his family home.

As before the war, Raoul was in no hurry to hold an exhibition, and it was only in May 1973 that some forty of his pictures – 'Equestrian Paintings and Sketches' – went on show at the Tryon Gallery, then in Dover Street. The show was well supported and almost everything sold, but not all the potential customers were easy to please. A woman who looked round the pictures said she would like to buy No 23, which depicted mares and foals trotting across an extensive landscape.

'Ah yes,' said the director of the gallery, 'one of his best. I believe he did it in France some years ago.'

'D'you mean to say these horses are *foreign*' exclaimed the woman in disgust. 'I would only ever buy pictures of English horses' – with which she floated round the walls once more and disappeared through the swing doors into the street.

Like echoes from the distant past, commissions still came in from hunts which wanted portraits of their masters, with their hounds, for presentation to the subjects when they retired or moved on. Two such were Rob Berkeley, Master of the Berkeley from 1928 to 1969, whom Raoul portrayed in the hunt's distinctive yellow coat, with the squat bulk of Berkeley Castle in the background, and Captain Ronnie Wallace, Master of the Heythrop from 1952 to 1977.

One of his last commissions came in 1977, the year of the Queen's silver jubilee, when he was asked to paint a picture of Her Majesty arriving on the racecourse at Ascot in the state carriage after the ceremonial drive from Windsor Great Park. The project demanded a considerable amount of research, first at the scene to be depicted and then at Windsor, where the state carriage was kept.

Raoul's first move was to sketch the entrance to the course at which the royal party would arrive. This he conceived to be the Golden Gates, and he spent two days drawing them, but then, to his chagrin, discovered that they were the wrong ones. Belatedly he realised that there were two sets of Golden Gates, old and new, and it was the new ones which he wanted, so that he had to start all over again.

At Windsor he was more fortunate, for he had a good friend in the form of Lieutenant-Colonel Sir John Miller, Crown Equerry, with whom he had served in the Brigade of Guards. Miller brought out everything for him – the carriage, the horses harnessed up, the postillions in their finery – and Raoul made three or four visits to capture all the detail correctly. In the end he painted two versions of the picture, the carriage and horses very much the same in both, but with different backgrounds.

The arrangement was that the paintings would be presented to the Queen at the Ascot meeting; she would choose one, and the other would go to the Stewards' Dining Room on the racecourse.

The authorities had promised Raoul that he would not have to appear when the presentation was made, but at the meeting he found himself being ushered into the Royal Box, where both pictures stood on easels. When the Queen said she could not make up her mind which to have, Raoul replied, 'If I were you, Ma'am, I wouldn't have either.'

'Oh God!' she exclaimed. 'You artists are all the same. You don't take life seriously.'

Being an expert on harness, she looked closely at one of the paintings and said, 'Don't you think that rein's a bit thin?' – whereupon Raoul drew out a ball-point pen and moved towards the easel.

'*What are you doing*?' cried the Queen in consternation; but Raoul carried on and quickly gave the rein a bit more substance. One picture is now in the Queen's private collection at Sandringham, the other at Ascot.

Raoul with his labrador Leo outside Westcote in 1988. As he grew older his paintings became smaller and more impressionistic, but he continued working in his studio well into his tenth decade.

OPPOSITE:
'Picnic'. Raoul never went to the seaside if he could avoid it, and this view of North Cornish headlands is perhaps an echo of visits to Lenarth, a famous West Country woodcock shoot.

LEFT:
Tumbler pigeons flying from the loft of the studio at Westcote. At one time numerous, they were later wiped out by sparrowhawks, and Raoul fired numerous verbal salvoes at the RSPB, complaining about the excessive protection afforded to raptors.

Death in the afternoon: a barn owl snatches a water vole from the surface of a pond as evening closes in.

CHAPTER ELEVEN

LOOKING BACK

In the sixth book of the *Iliad* there occurs one of Homer's most famous lines. As the armies manoeuvre before Troy, the Lycian leader Glaucus recalls the instructions with which his father despatched him to the war: αἰεν ἀριστευειν και ὑπειροχον ἐμμεναι ἀλλων (Always to be best, and pre-eminent above the rest). Yet the second word, *aristeuein* carries echoes beyond 'to be best'. It can also mean 'to behave well', and 'to conduct oneself in an aristocratic manner'.

In his life and career Raoul has surely taken Glaucus's watchword for his own. He has conducted matters as he has wished, deliberately cultivating the image of the high-born artist, living well, dressing well, painting well, secure in his own domain. Enemies, if he had any, might accuse him of being selfish, of always doing what he wanted. They might also say that he was lucky in that he married two rich women. Yet any attempt to criticise him would be undermined by his modesty, his generosity, his boyish sense of humour and his charm.

Even in his eighties and nineties women still found him devastating. Wong Farquhar, his picture framer in later years, declares herself besotted by him, 'the most charming man I've ever met, with the most perfect manners'. His particular gift, she notices, is 'his ability to make you feel you're the only person in the world he's ever been interested in'.

His second show at the Tryon took place in 1982, and he continued to paint all through his eighties; a magnificent picture done in 1985, of two stallions fighting, one black, one white, bears witness to the enduring vitality of his imagination. A chronic insomniac, he would often return to work after dinner and paint far into the night.

Yet that same year fate dealt him a heavy blow. Until then Kay had always been perfectly well. She hated the idea of growing old, and on documents she persistently entered her date of birth as 1918 rather than 1916, but she had had no serious medical problems. Then suddenly she began to drop things and suffer blackouts. On a beautiful day in August Karol took her into hospital in

Cheltenham and left her there while she drove home to fetch her things. When she and Raoul returned a couple of hours later, they met a doctor coming out of Kay's room. 'She's fine,' he told them. 'We've done all our tests. She'll be in for the night, but she can go home tomorrow.' Then Karol walked into the room and found her mother dead of a heart attack.

Raoul was so shattered that he could not even enter the room to say goodbye. Back at home, he withdrew into his shell, and for the next five years he simply did not mention Kay to anyone, not even to Karol, who was living next door and present every day. 'My life was at an end,' he wrote later. And yet his great spirit gradually fought its way back to the surface.

Living close to Westcote, Mike and Wong Farquhar had got to know him well. Then in the late 1970s they moved to Wiltshire, and when they started framing pictures as a hobby, Raoul asked them to do some of his. The experiment was a success, and led to the idea that they should hold a show of his paintings in their small gallery at home. Yet when they went over to Westcote to make a selection, they learned a sharp lesson.

'Oh!' exclaimed Mike, coming on something which he admired. 'That's wonderful.'

'You like it?' Raoul was instantly delighted. 'Do have it, then', and he forced it on them as a present. Mike felt highly embarrassed, and thereafter took care to be economical with his praise.

Any human being who reaches the age of ninety with faculties unimpaired is something of a phenomenon. Raoul passed that landmark in astonishing shape, still painting and exhibiting, still driving his Jaguar, still downing every pheasant with the first barrel. Mike Farquhar remembers a typical incident in the shooting field. As the guns were walking up a valley between drives, one of them, who had emphysema, began to lag behind. Raoul, noticing him, hurried back and said, 'Do let me take your gun and cartridge-bag' – even though he was ninety, and the other man nearly twenty years his junior.

Until he was ninety-two, Raoul continued to go for a short jog every day. Thereafter, he recorded, 'like the Edwardian yuppie,

I count my ties and I change my kit,
And the exercise keeps me awfully fit.'

An Edwardian is what he has remained – in his appearance, his dress, and his hankering after a more gracious, more leisurely past. In particular he hankers after Africa as it was in the days when he hunted big-game with his father; he laments the fact that modern vehicles, helicopters and radios have removed the excitement and danger from safaris, and put the nearest bar and restaurant just a mobile telephone call away.

Naturally, many of his memories are connected with hunting, stalking and shooting. Thinking back over the dogs he owned, he remembers all with affection, from Beetle, a black cocker spaniel which rode with him on his motorbike 'with his front paws on the handlebars and his ears flapping in my face', through Amber, Honey, Kipper (a lunatic Hungarian pointer) and Sooty to Ness, his latest labrador, who 'looks like a black seal'. Raoul described her as 'the best burglar alarm in the country', because if anyone or anything moves at night within 150 yards of the house, she sets up a blood-curdling racket. If Ness is slightly plumper than she should be, it is hardly surprising, for at meals her master's habit is to eat a small portion of his helping and then put the plate on the floor.

His innate modesty does not preclude him from claiming a few esoteric records:

1. I once shot a snipe which rose from a derelict double-decker London bus lying on its side in the back garden of a house in South Uist.
2. In Spain I shot a partridge with a policeman's revolver.
3. I was shot twice in one day by a canon of the Church.

With plenty of time to consider the idiocies of the modern world, he amuses himself by writing satirical sketches and collecting ridiculous newspaper headlines: 'EX-FIREMAN'S WIFE ASSAULTS POSTMAN WITH BREAKFAST KIPPER', 'TOADS ARE RIGHT-HANDED' etc. Most of his mockery is good-natured, but he has a few real *bêtes noires*, among them 'mush-room millionaires', with more money than sense or manners, particularly if they massacre low-flying pheasants by the thousand and consider themselves sportsmen. His pet hate, however, is the Royal Society for the Protection of Birds which, he reckons, has effectively killed off the songbirds in his garden by giving excessive protection to birds of prey, principally sparrowhawks. Savagely ironic letters to the RSPB evoke emollient answers but do not bring his lost finches and blackbirds back to life.

It is amusing to find that in his literary *jeux d'esprit* Raoul hits exactly the same note as his father. Just as Johnny, recovering from fever in the Sudan in 1924, wrote a cod travel brochure for the village of Rumbek – a ghastly place – under the name 'Professor Fathead, FRS', so Raoul constantly invents Beachcomber-ish characters like Lord Howlong of Hopover, 'who made a fortune in zip fasteners during the last war', and Sir George Springy, Chairman of the Worshipful Company of Shock-Absorbers.

Occasionally he bursts into verse with a jaunty limerick:

Said the Duchess of Alba to Goya,
'Remember that I'm your employa.'
So he painted her twice,
Once dressed very nice,
And once in the nude to annoya.

Over the years his contempt for trendy modern art has never wavered. He was once enraged when, in a London gallery, he saw a large white canvas with a single black line drawn across the centre and a red square in one top corner. On learning that the work had been sold the day before for £45,000, he told the gallery owner, 'That's obscene.'

'Don't be silly,' came the answer. 'If I'd asked for £500 – which we know the picture isn't worth – the man would have walked out of the building.'

The experience proved Raoul's point exactly: that gimmickry is everything, and that all too often talent, training and hard graft count for nothing. His special contempt is reserved for painters like Rothko, 'who covers vast areas of canvas with red paint and places a large black blob in the middle', or Jackson Pollock, 'who staggers about over the floor-covering dripping colours at random from tins with holes punched in the bottom'.

As for critics who take up some worthless artist for social or intellectual reasons, for them he has nothing but derision, and he lets off steam by composing reviews of the latest exhibitions: 'The fluid serenity of his pre-crustacean period . . . He has brought to our notice the artistic possibility of exhumation . . .'

He recalls with satisfaction the numerous occasions on which critics have been duped – not least by Munnings, who once tied a brush full of paint to a donkey's tail and backed the animal up against a canvas, so that its switching appendage created wild patterns which critics later proclaimed to be a masterpiece. Reflecting on artists in general, he points out that great talent has been shared by men of astonishingly diverse personalities:

Benvenuto Cellini was some sort of terrorist *manqué*, poor Van Gogh a nut-case, Velasquez a *hidalgo*, Augustus John an alcoholic, Toulouse-Lautrec a cripple. Those splendid Dutchmen must have included diplomats and courtiers like Rubens and Van Dyck. Many portrait painters must have been adept in the arts of sycophancy and flattery.

131

But where are the girls? Until this century almost without exception it has been a man's world. I would love to have seen the faces of the Pre-Raphaelite brotherhood if they had been asked to accept a female into their closed shop.

As a warning to aspiring artists, he once wrote:

If you are a professional painter or sculptor, you must realise that during your lifetime you may gain very little recognition. It is not a question of how much talent you have been blessed with: more a matter of how good your connections are with the publicity scene . . . Anything vaguely connected with sport is anathema to the *avante-garde* art critic. I personally find this very gratifying. And yet, however good or bad you are, do not despair. Painting is a wonderful therapy.

But it is in letters to friends that Raoul's sense of humour comes into its own. Epistles in big, bold handwriting and bronze ink radiate from Westcote (often styled 'Weskit') to all points of the compass, flying out like sparks from a Catherine wheel, and often ending, 'May your shadow never grow less.' One April, after the Farquhars had been to lunch and accidentally carried off a napkin, he wrote to Wong,

Milady,
I do thank you for returning the Westcote napery. I have spent the morning in the silver cupboard, counting the spoons, and am happy to inform you that nothing is missing. May I suggest that your distinguished husband should not be allowed to enter Marks & Spencer or Tesco unaccompanied? We do not want any unpleasantness in the Press, do we?
Yr. humble servant,
Leonardo da Weskit.

In October 1990, after a shoot with his friend Bobby Wills, he wrote to Mike:

Yesterday we accounted for 74 brace of partridges at Farmington. I fired eleven shots, but was fortunate to be next gun to your brother, who fired simultaneously and shouted 'Good shot!' The host, as usual, shot sixty brace, having cooked the draw.

For reasons impossible to divine, he invests some correspondents with pseudo-religious status, addressing them as 'Reverend' or 'Your Reverence'. One such is Christopher Fleming, another shooting friend and as irreligious as they come, who, on the envelope, often becomes 'The Bishop of Berks' or 'The Rev. C. Fleming, VAT', with 'If undelivered please return to the

Archbishop of Canterbury' scribbled on the back. In one such epistle, Raoul wrote:

Dear Sir,
The Hon. R. Wills [Bobby] came slumming at Westcote last week, and I am concerned that it may take him some time to recover from his traumatic experience in Kenya. I hear that not only did he think a cow-elephant made a serious pass at him, but that he was menaced by two hippos through the window of his minibus . . . He tells me his new Jaguar is too big, which must be an added strain . . .
I have just read that a lady twice knocked her husband out with a rolling pin. I am relieved to hear your glorious memsahib only uses a rolled-up *Times* . . . About 200 people passed through here at Easter. The cellar is empty.
Your constant admirer,
Charlie Creep.

Laughter and the love of friends have certainly kept Raoul going. So, even more, has the family. His three sons and one step-daughter have between them produced fourteen grandchildren. Among an ever-rising horde of great-grandchildren, the eldest are already in their teens. All constantly descend on Westcote, where the patriarch presides like a genial old lion at the centre of his pride. Fortified by generous draughts of whisky and champagne, fawned on by Ness, cherished by a devoted couple – Mary, the housekeeper-cook, and her husband Peter, master of all trades – he sits lapped by a sea of paintings, drawings, books and photograph albums.

The portrait of his mother, done when he was nineteen, hangs beside the fireplace, straight in front of his favourite chair. His glorious picture of Greyskin, who so nearly killed him, is by the door. Looking back from the age of ninety-six is like being on the summit of Everest: the view over years gone by is colossal, and it is inevitable that Raoul should now and then mourn the disappearance of people and things dear to him. Sometimes he cannot help but feel, as he himself wrote in a haunting phrase, 'the wind has blown the past away'.

INDEX

Figures in italics refer to pictures or captions